Talleyrand

BORN: February 2, 1754
DIED: May 16, 1838

Talleyrand was born an aristocrat and would have
been known as Prince Talleyrand except for an accident that crippled him. Custom prevented a cripple
from inheriting his father's title. Embittered and to
make up for his physical defect, young Charles decided to become powerful, rich and superior to all
around him. He succeeded far beyond his own
dreams as a statesman and diplomat. During the upheaval in France which brought Napoleon to power,
Talleyrand made the most of his opportunities. He
shaped the policies that made Napoleon Emperor of
France, and it was he who dictated the terms of Napoleon's banishment, when disaster followed his invasion of Russia. During Talleyrand's long life, he
served as an important link between the old world
and the world that gave birth to the democracies
of Europe.

Books by Manuel Komroff

TALLEYRAND

by

Manuel Komroff

JULIAN MESSNER
NEW YORK

Published by Julian Messner
Division of Pocket Books, Inc.
8 West 40 Street, New York 10018

Second Printing, 1966

Printed in the United States of America

Library of Congress Catalog Card No. 65-12954

Acknowledgment

Talleyrand lived to be eighty-four, and his long span of years, 1754 to 1838, were years of historical upheavals. These were the dramatic years which ushered in the bloody French Revolution, witnessed the rise of Napoleon, the collapse of his empire, and the return of the Bourbons to the throne of France. These were the years that bridged the old world, the feudal world of aristocracy, with the new world, the world that saw the rise of the common man and democracy. The vast historical research and organization required for this slim volume would not have been possible without the assistance of my wife, Odette Komroff, who also shared in the writing of this book.

M. K.

Contents

Contents

Talleyrand

1.

Alone in a Changing World

❧

Charles Maurice de Talleyrand-Périgord, one of the most brilliant and powerful statesmen in all history, was born in Paris on February 2, 1754. Louis XV was on the throne of France, and Charles' parents, Charles Daniel and Alexandrine de Talleyrand, being of the nobility served at the court at Versailles.

The Talleyrands were an old and aristocratic family who came from Périgord, a small province in southwestern France just north of Bordeaux. Old records claimed that they were directly descended from the Counts of Périgord who served Charlemagne. During the past three or four centuries, they were included in that very fortunate group of nobles who served the kings of France as honored members of the court.

Talleyrands were members of the royal court of Louis XIII. Other members of the family served at court during the golden age of Louis XIV. And the parents of the newborn Charles Maurice were part of the glittering court of Louis XV. They served faithfully, even though it was always a hardship, for they were without fortune, and keeping up a façade of splendor was very costly.

It was, perhaps, this devotion to the King and the great pride that Charles Daniel and Alexandrine de Talleyrand took in their aristocrat position, pride marching hand in hand with shabby poverty, that caused them to shamefully neglect their little son. They provided Charles with no home life, no parental affection, no loving care, no intimate playful hours. In fact, immediately following his birth, Charles was boarded out with a poor woman who lived in the suburbs of Paris.

Denied his parents' love, little Charles was destined to suffer still further. Before he reached the age of four, he was crippled for life. The woman in whose charge he had been placed sat him one day on the top of a table from which he fell, seriously injuring his right foot. Frightened by what had happened, or because of her dismal ignorance, she did not report the injury to anyone until it was too late to have it corrected. The result was that Talleyrand spent the rest of his long life with a badly deformed foot and a very painful leg which had to be supported by a heavy iron brace. He was unable to walk except with the aid of a cane.

It was a cruel fate to be thus condemned at such an early age, yet this accident brought Charles the only happiness he was to know during his childhood. His maternal great-grandmother, the Princess de Chalais, who lived on the family estates in Périgord, learning of how the child was neglected, offered to take complete charge of him. Glad to be released from all responsibility, his parents immediately sent him off alone by coach. It was a hard seventeen-day journey.

The Princess de Chalais was a fine old lady and she showered her attention, her kindness and affection on little Charles Maurice. For the first time in his life he knew the warmth of love and what it was to live in a home of which he was really a part.

It was also here at his great-grandmother's that Charles Maurice first learned what it meant to be an aristocrat. Here he first enjoyed the luxuries and pleasures to which his birth entitled him, for in the home of the Princess de Chalais he lived in the midst of the old world of French aristocracy, a world which was soon to disappear.

In his great-grandmother's château there gathered all the more educated and enlightened people of the province, gentlemen and ladies of rank as well as men of the Church. There were even occasional visitors from far distant Paris. During the afternoons and evenings, sitting on a stool at the feet of this noble old lady, little Charles heard discussions on art, music, philosophy and politics.

He knew true happiness living with his great-grandmother in Périgord, but this was soon to be taken from him. After only three and a half years, when he was eight, his parents asked that he be returned to Paris. They felt that it was time for him to enter school. And so he was cruelly parted from his beloved great-grandmother.

Alone, the grieving little boy again took the long journey. But even after reaching Paris he found no solace for his sorrow. His parents were not there to meet him. Neither his mother nor his father cared enough to come. Indeed, Talleyrand later recorded that up to that time his father had never laid eyes on him! They had sent an old valet to await the coach and take the little boy directly to the College d'Harcourt where they had already enrolled him.

Although this school was only a short distance from the Talleyrands' home, during the seven years that Charles spent there he was allowed to come home to dinner, with an in-

structor, only once each week. These evenings were always
strained and formal, and his father bid him good-by each
time with the same cheerless words, "Be good, my boy, and
do as you are told." Many years later as Talleyrand looked
back upon his bleak childhood he wrote, "I am perhaps the
only man of distinguished birth and belonging to a numerous
and highly esteemed family who never enjoyed, for a week
of his life, the joy of living beneath the paternal roof."

There is still further proof of his parents' indifference to
him. One day Charles was taken ill with the most dreaded of
illnesses, smallpox. All his parents did was to send a sedan
chair so that he could be transported from the school to another part of Paris where a certain woman ran a small in-
firmary. No one came to see him. No one inquired about his
progress. However, in spite of this neglect and the severity of
both his case and the treatment, he recovered. He has recorded that he was bundled into a bed, the bed curtains were
drawn, a roaring fire was built, and he was fed steaming hot
drinks to "excite" his fever.

Being unloved by his parents naturally caused Charles
much suffering; however, many years later he was able to find
some virtue in his parents' heartless attitude. He wrote, "The
lack of interest shown in me . . . saddened me. I felt helpless
and always thrown upon myself. But I will not complain of
having to suffer so early in life. To it I owe a capacity for
serious reflection and calm judgment in misfortune."

These words prove that as a mature man Talleyrand was
finally able to accept his parents' cruel indifference. There
was, however, one expression of their rejection of him for
which he never forgave them. Its bitterness colored his entire
life. It happened when his studies at Harcourt drew to an end.

Being the Talleyrands' eldest living son, Charles Maurice

was heir to the title of Prince and whatever properties his parents possessed. But because he was a cripple his parents decided to deny him his rightful heritage and bestow it instead upon another son who had recently been born to them. They felt justified in doing this because for centuries it had been the tradition in the Talleyrand family for the eldest son to follow a military career and serve the king of France as commander of one of his regiments. No cripple could aspire to such glory!

It was a bitter experience. But what made it even more odious to the growing boy was that his parents, to get rid of him and have him safely out of the way, told him that he was to enter the Church and become a priest.

Charles protested. Young as he was he knew that he was not meant for a religious life. But his parents, especially his mother, a very religious woman, could not be swayed. Instead of serving the king of France, Charles Maurice would serve God, and she and his father spared no effort to paint a rosy picture of Charles' future career. They told him that as an aristocrat he could easily rise to a high position in the Church. There were many Church dignitaries who lived in great splendor. He had only to think of his good uncle, Alexander, who was assistant to the Archbishop of Rheims. He lived in the greatest of opulence. . . . Yes, it was settled Charles was to become a priest.

Charles Maurice was fifteen when he finished his studies at the College d'Harcourt. Dressing him in a cassock, his parents then sent him to stay with his uncle, Alexander de Talleyrand, Coadjutor to the Archbishop of Rheims. They hoped that the monk's robe they had put on him and the beauty and mystery of the great and ancient cathedral would inspire the

St. Sulpice: "Five long, sad years of bad humor, silence and reading." He remembered himself as "an extremely unhappy and wrathful young man."

In an effort to escape from his unhappiness, he plunged into the world of books. Spending long hours in the college library, he devoured the works of important historians and found great distraction, even inspiration, in the biographies of famous statesmen. He also read classical literature and philosophy. And the more he read, the more the world opened up before him and the more he became determined to carve a career for himself that was independent of the Church.

His revolt against his heartless parents, and their attempt to force him to become a priest, expressed itself in still another way. He defied all sense of propriety for a seminary student by falling in love with a beautiful young actress who lived a few doors away from his "prison." Whenever he could, which was surprisingly often, he visited with her in her home.

During Talleyrand's fifth year at St. Sulpice, Louis XV died and the twenty-year-old Louis XVI and the eighteen-year-old Marie Antoinette became King and Queen of France. Because of his noble birth and his parents' position at court, Talleyrand was one of those favored with an invitation to attend the coronation, which took place in the Cathedral at Rheims, a place he knew so well.

There, for the first time, the young man witnessed a royal pageant, a ceremony of dazzling splendor attended by the royalty and high dignitaries of many lands. This was his first introduction into the great world, the world of power, the world of kings, queens and princes, the world in which he would himself soon play a leading role.

The reign of Louis XIV is known as the Period of the Rising Sun and its emblem is a golden sunburst. The rising sun symbolizes the brilliance of Louis XIV's court and the flowering at this time of French art and literature. It was then that Versailles was built, that French wall decoration, tapestries, furniture and weaving of carpets reached their greatest height. It was then that the Comédie Française was founded and that Corneille, Racine, Boileau and Molière produced their great works.

The reign of Louis XV, on the other hand, is known as the Age of Reason, for it was during his years upon the throne that France seethed with new and startling social ideas, ideas which filled the air with excitement and which hastened the French Revolution. The men who presented these ideas have become famous in world history; the influence of their thought is still felt today.

The first of these world-shaking men was the great jurist, Montesquieu. In his first book, *The Persian Letters,* he cleverly criticized the society of the time by representing it as seen through the eyes of two Persians traveling through Europe. This biting satire introduced a literary form through which one could criticize outworn laws, the aristocracy, the Church and the king, without running the risk of being arrested for inciting the people against their government.

The Persian Letters was tremendously daring and popular, and in the years that followed, Montesquieu wrote several other provocative books. However, his most important work was his last, called *The Spirit of Laws.* In this great work Montesquieu studied human society and weighed it in the scales of justice. He was a bitter enemy of intolerance and despotism, and he brought attention to the virtues of the English constitutional monarchy and its democratic character. In fact, after the publication of *The Spirit of Laws,* English democracy became a favorite subject of conversation in fashionable European circles, for Montesquieu's works were so stimulating that they were read not only in France but throughout Europe. They were also read in America and *The Spirit of Laws* played a definite role in the writing of the United States Constitution.

Montesquieu died the year following Talleyrand's birth; but the ferment generated by his ideas influenced French thought very deeply throughout Talleyrand's youth and the boy's thinking was definitely colored by it.

The second great figure of the Age of Reason was Voltaire with his bold attacks on politics, education and the Church. He reached his greatest power and popularity during the years when Talleyrand was growing into manhood. He did not die until Talleyrand was twenty-four years of age. Young Talleyrand was so deeply influenced by Voltaire's thought that he practically worshipped him—a thoroughly unaccepable thing for a theological student to do. In fact, his admiration of Voltaire was such that one day when the famous philosopher came to Paris, Talleyrand attended a great affair held in his honor and, being overcome by the sight of his idol, came forward, knelt and asked Voltaire for his blessing. The old man, then about eighty-four, solemnly bestowed his blessing upon Talleyrand amid the loud applause of all those assembled.

Voltaire's ideas were the embodiment of eighteenth-century "enlightenment." His writings helped bring on the French Revolution. In fact, it was only seven years after his death that the Bastille, where he himself had been imprisoned several times for his radical ideas, was destroyed by a mob of the Revolution.

Montesquieu and Voltaire were the two giants of the Age of Reason, but there were others who also wielded tremendous influence. Rousseau and Diderot were among these.

Rousseau ushered in a period of romanticism. He believed in the natural goodness of man and felt that man-made institutions were evil and had a corrupting influence upon society. He advocated a return to "simple living," a return to "nature." His philosophy was so popular, especially among the aristocracy, that gentlemen and ladies all over France dressed themselves as shepherds and shepherdesses and tried to give up their jaded ways in spite of the fact that they still used silk instead of homespun. Even the Queen, Marie Antoinette, joined the movement. She had a small farm, Le Petit Trianon, built close to the palace at Versailles and, dressed as a dairymaid, went there almost daily with her ladies-in-waiting to milk the cows.

Rousseau's "back to nature" philosophy had its light, gay side, but he also presented other ideas which troubled the deep waters of social order. "Why is it," he asked, "that Man is born free and yet everywhere he is in chains?" And it was Rousseau who first wrote those three words which became the slogan of the Revolution, words which are today carved into the stone of many public buildings in France, words which express the essence of France. It was Rousseau who wrote, "Liberty, Equality, Fraternity."

The fourth great figure of the Age of Reason was Diderot, the novelist, dramatist and philosopher, who enlisted all the important French writers of the day to contribute to an encyclopedia he was compiling.

Diderot was a man of original ideas and he admired originality in others. He, therefore, wanted to gather together in his encyclopedia all the new philosophies which were then being presented. He felt that these new ideas, which were stirring the very depths of society, combined into one great work, would produce a tremendously powerful social force.

Diderot was right. When his encyclopedia appeared it shook the very foundations of the existing social order by clearly asserting some simple democratic ideas. It stated, for instance, that the government's first concern should be for the common people and that all efforts should be made to encourage scientific knowledge and to keep the nation at peace.

Such ideas seem almost childish to modern men, but in those days the Church and the State were both still dominated by medieval concepts. The Church subordinated all scientific thought to religious thought and the State believed in absolutism and militarism. It is no wonder that the encyclopedia was immediately condemned as a conspiracy against society and Diderot was imprisoned for six months.

However, since it is impossible to stop the flow of ideas with prison bars, the philosophies presented in the encyclopedia continued to spread, and Diderot's great work became one of the most important factors in fomenting the French Revolution.

The Age of Reason electrified France and changed the whole course of French history. In fact, its force was so great that it changed all European history. Its philosophies crossed the wide Atlantic and fired the patriots of the American Revolution. The opening shots fired at Lexington, Concord and Bunker Hill and the naming of George Washington as Commander-in-Chief all took place in 1775, the very year that the Age of Reason came to an end and Louis XVI was crowned King of France.

Four years later the fruits of reason were being gathered in

the United States, where with the aid of Lafayette, French
troops, ships and money, the American Revolution was drawing to a successful end. The King of France had already recognized the independence of the United States and the people
of France were stirred and happy.

The first twenty-one years of Talleyrand's life were lived
during the Age of Reason and its swift current of ideas helped
to mold this neglected, lonely and unhappy youth. He sensed
that something very important, perhaps violent, was imminent. He was eager to play a part in the new world which he
felt was about to be born. But having learned as a very small
boy to accept life as it happened, and being penniless, he did
not dare defy his parents, especially his religious mother, and
go off on his own. Without money he was helpless; and so,
having completed five years at the seminary of St. Sulpice, he
now became a student in the theological school at the Sorbonne.

Talleyrand had four more years of study before he could
enter the priesthood. However, he found the Sorbonne much
more to his taste than St. Sulpice. He had more freedom; he
could choose theological courses that were comparatively easy
and he had plenty of free time to make friends and attend
parties. In fact, he now entered a life of complete liberty.

His parents and his instructors knew that he was leading
a very free life, but they did not say a word. It was a time of
extreme moral laxity, and everyone accepted behavior in seminary students which would not be tolerated today. All France
—its aristocrats, the government and the Church—was rid-
dled with corruption. The times were so corrupt that even
the King played a part in leading Talleyrand on his wayward
path.

Louis XVI was particularly fond of Talleyrand's father, Charles Daniel de Talleyrand, because he had served his grandfather, Louis XV, and was a close friend of his late father, the Dauphin and only son of Louis XV. So when Charles Daniel de Talleyrand asked him to grant his young son, who was destined for the Church, a benefice, the King did so without the least hesitation. He gave the twenty-one-year-old Charles Maurice, who had not yet taken any major vows, charge of the Abbey of St. Denis at Rheims with an income of 18,000 livres a year! In our money this would amount to only $3,600, but in the purchasing power of the time it was the equivalent of $10,000.

The King's generous gesture pleased Charles beyond all measure, but it also helped in his corruption. Seeing how easily money could come to a man of the Church who had the right connections, he suddenly decided to do as his parents wanted and become a priest. Not only would he become a priest; he would also become a bishop and live like the Archbishop of Rheims. He might even someday become a cardinal!

Talleyrand had suddenly learned the evil lesson his parents had tried so hard to force upon him. He was no longer the honest boy of fifteen who had been sent to Rheims to live in the splendor and luxury of the Archbishop's mansion. He now understood clearly how "one could enter a profession with the intention of following another."

His position at Rheims carried with it no duties, and he remained in Paris, where he continued his theological studies at the Sorbonne and where he now led the life he chose. With money one could do anything. He rented a very attractive apartment, bought the most fashionable clothes and plunged into the gayest life that Paris and Versailles could offer. It was at this time that he also became a frequent visitor at gambling houses.

Talleyrand's behavior was certainly shocking for one studying for the priesthood. In fact, he seems to have done only one honorable thing at this period. He remembered his tutor at St. Sulpice, a man whom his parents had not paid during four long years, and he corrected this injustice.

Talleyrand became a subdeacon on August 12, 1775, and a deacon on September 17, 1779. Three months later he was ordained a priest.

His uncle, Alexander, was now Archbishop, Duke of Rheims. Since it was the wish of this now all-powerful man to ordain his nephew, Talleyrand journeyed to Rheims. But his soul was torn by the agony of doubt.

The night before the solemn ceremony was to take place, he wept. A friend tried to comfort him and persuade him to turn his back upon the priesthood, but he kept repeating, "It is too late. It is too late. There is no turning back. . . . They want to make a priest of me! Well, you'll see, they'll make me into something really frightful!"

It was a dreary December day when Talleyrand took his final vows in the chapel of the famous Cathedral at Rheims. He was twenty-five years old. Returning to Paris, his heart still weighted with misgivings, he confided to a friend, "They forced me to become a priest and, you will see, they'll regret it."

2.

The Abbé de Périgord

❖

The Abbé de Périgord, as Talleyrand was now known, was welcomed everywhere. His distinguished family name opened the doors of society. But he had more than his name—he had breeding and polished manners. He was highly educated, and when he spoke, his ideas were interesting and his humor often biting. He understood the art of conversation and could hold his listeners spellbound.

Men were pleased to be in his company. Women adored him. He, therefore, entered fully and freely into the rich, decadent life of the French aristocracy. He attended elegant dinners and salons, went to the opera and theater, flirted with titled ladies and played whist for high stakes with princes.

However, he did not trail a priest's cassock over the polished floors of the Parisian palaces. No, not Talleyrand. He dressed in the fashion of the day. An artist who painted his portrait at this time shows him in a loose blue velvet coat with wide lapels, a white waistcoat, full lawn cravat, flesh-colored knee breeches and silk stockings and simple slippers. His hair, in accordance with the fashion of the day, is fairly long and covers his ears.

Talleyrand was of slight build and medium height; he looked rather frail, although he had tremendous energy. His features were delicate. He had large blue-gray eyes and his nose was slightly upturned, giving accent to a haughty expression, an expression that almost hinged on insolence. It was an expression that revealed nothing of his inner thoughts and feelings, neither surprise, pleasure nor anger. In later years, his enemies were to say that he concealed the heart of a devil under an angel's face.

His bearing made up for his defects. He carried himself with such ease and proud distinction that some said he actually limped with grace.

Talleyrand enjoyed every moment he spent in the rich aristocratic world and decided to live in the same manner as his friends. Only one thing prevented him from doing so—he lacked money. Undaunted, he decided to become rich, very rich, and having made up his mind, he immediately set out to achieve this end.

Being attracted to finance and feeling that he had a talent for administration, he lost no time placing his name before the Assembly of the Clergy and winning an appointment as one of the two Agents-General of the Church, an office which concerned itself with the business management of Church properties as well as with problems arising between the clergy and the government. The year was 1780.

It was the kind of official position that demanded little time or effort, but Talleyrand saw in it a chance to meet men in high government positions, men who could later be of use to him. He was eager to impress these men with his knowledge, his ability and his ideas for reforms. And this is just what he did.

The King's chief ministers were astonished by the way the young Abbé de Périgord grasped hold of the most intricate and serious problems. They were amazed at his ability to suggest practical solutions. To his great satisfaction, he learned that his name kept recurring in their conversations.

In his first political maneuver, Talleyrand succeeded in winning the attention and good will of the King's ministers. But that was not all. He also succeeded in pleasing the Church. The State, because of the shocking extravagances of the court, the expenses of helping the American Revolution and the inability of the poverty-stricken peasants to pay taxes, was rapidly going bankrupt. The Church, on the other hand, was extremely rich. So the ministers of the King suggested that some of the Church's great wealth be turned over to the State. Talleyrand courteously said, "No." He had not been appointed Agent-General to give away property which belonged exclusively and irrevocably to the Church. On this he stood firm.

The Assembly of the Clergy that had elected Talleyrand in 1780 did not hold another congress until 1785; and once again, Talleyrand won the approval of his fellow Churchmen. He presented a report on education, which was completely in the hands of the Church, and suggested that it be made universal and compulsory; this so impressed those present that they immediately elected him as one of the two secretaries of the Assembly.

Naturally Talleyrand was very pleased with the high honor he had just received, but his good fortune was not yet to end. One of the archbishops present at the Assembly was so impressed by the young Abbé that he proposed that the Assembly recommend to His Majesty that Talleyrand be elevated to the rank of bishop as soon as a vacancy should occur!

Talleyrand was delighted at the prospect of becoming a bishop so soon. It would mean power and money, a great deal of money, and would serve as a steppingstone to bigger things. He would now surely stand a chance of becoming a cardinal.

However, the King did not comply with the wishes of the Assembly of the Clergy. His Majesty, who was very religious, had heard rumors about the Abbé de Périgord's interest in worldly pleasures such as wine, women and gambling, and he felt that the young priest did not display a sufficiently spiritual outlook to become a bishop. The King said that he hated to name bishops in whom "the Holy Ghost was a mere ghost."

The King's rejection caused Talleyrand the greatest disappointment, but he refused to accept defeat. If the King would not honor him, he would appeal directly to the Pope. He would not ask to be made a bishop, he would ask to be elevated to the high post of cardinal. That would give him real power, real wealth. Through several of his friends, influential nobles connected with the court, negotiations were begun with the Vatican.

However, the whole scheme ended disastrously. Talleyrand never became a cardinal because the nobles who interceded for him in Rome disliked Marie Antoinette, who was an Austrian princess. She disliked them, too, and when she learned how they were going over the King's head and appealing to the Pope on behalf of their friend, she wrote to the Austrian Cardinal in the Vatican and the whole matter was dropped.

Nevertheless, after a reasonable lapse of time and when the whole unpleasant affair about the cardinal's hat was fading into the past, the King was again approached on behalf of the Abbé de Périgord. This time it was the old Charles Daniel de Talleyrand, who lying on his deathbed asked the King, as a last favor, to appoint his son, Charles Maurice de Talleyrand-Périgord as Bishop of Autun, a vacancy which had just occurred.

Louis XVI could not refuse his dying courtier, he who had been so loved by his father, and so he conceded to the request. He did even better than that; he also gave Charles Maurice charge of the Abbey of Cell in Poitou.

Charles Maurice was now not only a bishop but also the director of two abbeys with a combined income of 40,000 to 50,000 livres a year or $30,000 purchasing power. He was rich and he was powerful.

Talleyrand was now Bishop of Autun but he was not consecrated in Autun as he should have been. He was too busy with his gay life in Paris to bother taking the long trip to Autun for such a trifling matter. He merely wrote his flock a very respectful and moving letter, excusing himself on some pretext or other, and then went to Issy on the outskirts of Paris to take the solemn vows of bishop. His consecration took place on January 16, the opening month of that fateful year of 1789. Six months later the Bastille was stormed and torn apart by an angry mob.

France was charged with discontent. It was a time of intense social tension. The very ground seemed to rumble with the growls of the downtrodden people. In an attempt to pacify this discontent, the King, at the suggestion of Necker, his Minister of Finance, and his other advisers, decided to call together a representative body at Versailles to solve the financial dilemma facing the State and to quiet the social unrest by investigating the possibility of allowing the people some

sort of representation in the government. It was the first
national meeting to be called together in France since 1614
and was known as the Estates General, for it consisted of three
bodies: the Clergy or First Estate, the Nobility or Second
Estate, and the People or Third Estate.

Hearing of the King's plans for the Estates General, the
first in 175 years, Talleyrand was seized with a consuming
desire to be present. It fired his imagination. He had distinguished himself at the two sessions of the Assembly of the
Clergy and he very rightly reasoned that the Estates General
would provide him with a much larger stage on which to display his talents. At such an assembly he would meet all the
most important people of France. Besides, he considered himself eminently well suited to serve; being a bishop he knew
the Church, being a noble he knew the aristocracy, and having made a study of the educational system of France, he
knew the people. Who was better qualified?

He lost no time. Ordering his trunks packed and his coach
made ready at once for the long trip to Autun, he would ask
the priests of his diocese to elect him as their representative
to the First Estate. He showed no trace of embarrassment at
not having gone to Autun to be consecrated, no embarrassment at having neglected his sacred duties in preference for
gambling and the brilliant social life which Paris had to offer.
He was indeed proving that as a man of the Church he was
"something really frightful."

Arriving at Autun, Talleyrand called in his priests one or
two at a time and, after greeting each most warmly, sounded
them out concerning their opinions on national affairs. He
was surprised to find that his priests, like most priests in
France, sided with the people and felt that sweeping reforms

were needed. Having finally gathered all the material he needed, he wrote a paper incorporating the ideas he had just been given and read it to a gathering of his priests, saying that if they elected him to the Estates General this would be the program he would support.

His program was very democratic. It recommended that the Estates General become a permanent fixture, hold regular meetings and help the King and his ministers govern the land. It also recommended a codification of the law and asked that trial by jury and freedom of speech and of the press be guaranteed. No taxation should be imposed without the consent of the people. Free trade should be instituted. Reforms should be undertaken in the field of education so that the people, not just the rich and noble, could benefit. The country's desperate financial situation should be alleviated by sale of Crown lands and the floating of loans. And laws should be passed assuring everyone of the right to work, which he noted was "the only possession of those who have no property."

It was a radical manifesto and won the complete approval of his priests. They did not realize that for the most part Talleyrand was simply reading back to them what they had told him. They believed that these were also his ideas. They did not know that he was a conservative and was only using them to further his personal ambitions. They, therefore, elected him as their representative to the Estates General. His voice would be their voice. Through him they would help draw up some sort of document giving the people "rights." They instructed him "to work for a charter that will maintain the invariable rights of all . . ."

It was the eve of Easter. Spiritual duties should have kept the Bishop of Autun close to his cathedral there, but his trunks were packed and his coach was ready. There would be other Easters but not another gathering of the Estates General. His coach rolled on to Paris, to Versailles.

Talleyrand was about to brand his name upon events which would scorch the pages of history.

3.

The Revolution

❖

The Estates General convened at Versailles on May 5, 1789. Louis XVI had provided every possible convenience for the comfort of the delegates and his hopes were high as he welcomed them to the seat of the French government. However, from the opening hour, the three Estates became locked in a struggle which doomed the Estates General and led directly to the Revolution.

The question upon which the Estates could not agree concerned seating and voting. Should the three Estates sit together in one hall and poll each vote individually, or should each Estate meet in a separate hall and vote as a unit casting only one vote?

The First and Second Estates, or the Church and Nobility, wanted to meet separately and vote as units. Their interests were similar and their two votes combined could always outvote the single vote of the Third Estate, or the People.

The Third Estate, recognizing this obvious threat, insisted that the three Estates sit in one hall and that the delegates be polled individually. The Third Estate knew that most of the priests among the delegates of the First Estate and a few of the nobles of the Second Estate would vote with them and thereby guarantee victory for the Third Estate, which had six hundred votes to the three hundred votes of the First Estate and the three hundred votes of the Second Estate.

Such was the temper of the times that the battle raged on for six long weeks. The Church and the Nobles would not give in to the People. And the People were adamant.

At last on June 22, the First Estate, under pressure from the priests, gave in. However the Nobles still refused to surrender.

Then the King intervened. On June 23, siding with the Nobility, he expressed the wish that each Estate meet in separate halls and vote as a unit. To force the delegates to do as he said, he foolishly ordered the doors to the hall where the Estates had been battling locked.

Defying the King, the Third Estate immediately took possession of the building which housed the tennis courts, and swearing a solemn oath, the delegates vowed to remain there until their work was accomplished. If the First and Second Estates chose to join them, they were welcome; if not, they would proceed without them. The Third Estate assumed full sovereign power as representatives elected by the people and swore not to disband until a constitution was adopted guaranteeing the rights of man. They also formally adopted the name of National Assembly.

The King now capitulated. He ordered the Clergy and the Nobility to join the Third Estate, but he had acted too late. The people of France had reached the end of their patience. A constitution had been too long delayed. Mobs began gathering in the streets of Paris. A few weeks later, on July 14, 1789, a date as glorious to the French as July 4, 1776, is to the people of the United States, the people of Paris besieged the Bastille. This ugly prison, a symbol of oppression, intolerance and despotism, was torn apart stone by stone.

The French Revolution had begun. All over France the peasants followed the example set by the people of Paris. They stormed and burned the manor houses and châteaux of the aristocrats, and some aristocrats were murdered by the aroused people. The King was helpless. He had lost his authority, and his voice was no longer obeyed.

Many of the uncompromising Nobles and some of the high Churchmen left the Assembly, but it continued to meet. The delegates had sworn to carry through the work, and they were determined not to disband until they had drawn up a constitution that had been accepted by the King. Their enthusiasm was so great that in one evening, the evening of August 4, the Assembly passed one resolution and decree after another, abolishing every remnant of the feudal system. Within a few hours the people of France were freed forever from such ancient abuses as game laws benefiting the aristocrats, tithes, feudal courts of law, special military privileges for the rich and powerful, land tenure and serfdom.

However, as the hot summer wore on and in spite of the reforms, conditions grew worse each day. Money was scarce, and without money the people could not pay their taxes. The King was distraught, not at all sure of his next step. Finally he ordered his Minister of Finance to appeal to the rich to contribute to a "Patriotic Treasure Chest." The response was immediate and generous. Ladies and gentlemen threw all kinds of valuable things into the chest: jewelry, precious stones, fancy snuffboxes, watches, shoe buckles, old gold coins, things of silver and things of gold. Even the King and Queen contributed some gold plates and silver dishes of great value.

It was like a game. And in the fashionable salons of Paris

the great ladies, who had sacrificed their jewels, now adorned themselves with pieces of stone from the Bastille, which they had set in laurel leaves.

But the King's plan for saving the economy did not work, and in October another event occurred which changed the course of the Revolution and the work of the Assembly. Conditions had grown so bad that there was no food in Paris, and the women, crying for bread, marched the twelve miles to the palace at Versailles and defied the King's Guard to shoot them. They broke into the palace grounds and demanded that the King and his family return with them at once to Paris.

The King was powerless to resist. He rode from Versailles to Paris, his royal coach surrounded by the mob. With him were his Queen, Marie Antoinette, his sister and his two children. Behind the royal carriage came fifty carts loaded with grain, given as a peace offering by the King from his stores at Versailles.

The mob had decorated the royal carriage with the tricolor —the red, white and blue flag of the Revolution—and as they marched they sang. Pointing to the royal carriage and the line of provision wagons, they called out to those lining the roadway, "Courage, friends! We shall not want for bread now. We are bringing the baker, the baker's wife and the baker's little boy."

They led the King to the Tuileries. And from that moment on, although free to live in his splendid palace, Louis XVI was really a prisoner of the people.

Paris now became the capital of France. The Assembly moved from Versailles and established itself in the riding school next to the palace.

Talleyrand played no part in the struggle over the seating of the Estates General, but when most of the high Churchmen and Nobles walked out, he stayed behind with the priests and other clergymen who sided with the People. He was a realist and a conservative, not a reactionary or an extremist, or "Republican" as such people were then called. He admired the British constitutional monarchy and hoped that the same form of government could be devised for France. He felt that the People's demands for a constitution could no longer be delayed. He, therefore, joined with others who felt as he did and formed the "Center" at the National Assembly.

Talleyrand's faith in the People was badly shaken, however, when the Bastille was besieged. He deplored mob action and felt that the King should subdue the mob with armed force. Unless the King took a firm stand, warned Talleyrand, all would be lost.

The King refused to resort to bloodshed, and many aristocrats now fled the country. Talleyrand, however, chose to remain in France. He did this for two reasons. He had a deep love for France, and driven on by personal ambition, he wanted to play a part in reshaping her future.

Talleyrand planned to help draw up the constitution, but he felt that the desperate financial situation must be attended to before anything else. He had not forgotten that the original purpose in calling the Assembly was to find a way to avoid bankruptcy of the monarchy and find new resources for the nation. He deplored the King's ridiculous "Patriotic Treasure Chest," realizing that it was doomed to failure. He knew full well that the contributions would add up to only a fraction of the one hundred million livres needed to save the country. He was determined to find a real and lasting solution to the pressing problem. And he did.

Just one week after the hungry women of Paris marched on Versailles, the Bishop of Autun mounted the rostrum of the Assembly. He had a motion he wanted to propose.

Desperate situations call for desperate solutions, and Talleyrand knew that his proposal would be world-shaking. He did not avoid the issue but went directly to the point. He, who only a few years before had politely but firmly said "No" to the King's Minister of Finance when he suggested taking over Church properties, now proposed that the government do that very thing! Acting as though this idea was original with him, he began by recalling that in the long search for resources which could save the nation, one rich source had been overlooked. "This source," he said, "seems to me to be found entirely in Church properties."

A deathly hush fell over the Assembly. But Talleyrand, a product of the Age of Reason, appealed to the members with common sense and logic. He was an eloquent speaker and had the power of persuasion.

"The Church," he said, "is not a proprietor like other proprietors, because the property which it enjoys . . . was given to it by the faithful not for the benefit of the clergy but for the serving of certain functions. . . . Who really owns these Church lands? The answer can hardly be doubtful; the nation owns them. . . . They were indeed given to the Church . . . but the Church is not merely the clergy. . . . The Church is the whole body of the faithful; and the whole body of the faithful in a Catholic land, can it be anything but the nation?"

Talleyrand went on quietly and calmly. Having made it clear that in confiscating Church property, the people were only taking what already belonged to them, he then went on to explain that the transfer of wealth also imposed a transfer of obligations. These he listed. The State would now have to take over the administration of Church properties and maintain the hospitals, poorhouses, charities and schools. All buildings and churches would have to be kept in repair, and one hundred million livres would have to be put aside each year to pay the salaries of the clergy.

The idea of confiscating Church property was revolutionary in the extreme. But there was an even more revolutionary aspect to this proposal. Talleyrand's motion called for the transfer and control of charity, education and other such social functions from the Church to the State. For centuries these functions had been firmly held in the hands of the Church. The Church had always felt particularly strongly about education. It had always considered that the education of the young was its domain and even its sacred duty and that no one else had the right to invade this province.

Talleyrand knew the full import of his proposal. He knew it would bring about a conflict between the Church and the People. He knew that the Church would not surrender easily nor willingly, and he knew that he would be blamed for the rupture. He also knew that he would now have many enemies and probably be forced to resign as bishop.

However, Talleyrand had no intention of resigning—at least not yet. He wanted to remain a bishop as long as possible. He wanted to use for his own benefit, whatever prestige the title of bishop carried with it, and he needed the money which his high Church post provided. He had no other source of income. In other words, he wanted to put to full use that lesson in corruption which he had been taught as a child— that one could engage in a profession while also engaging in other interests that were diametrically opposed.

And so, playing both ends against the middle, he sent a letter to the curates of Autun asking them to pray to the

Lord to "remember a nation which has been dedicated" to Him since its very origin and, in this time of trouble, "to defend her cause."

The National Assembly passed Talleyrand's motion on confiscation of Church property, and as he had expected, he was renounced as a traitor by most of the clergy and nobles of France, even some of those sitting in the Assembly.

However, Talleyrand did not care too much. He was not a religious person and, therefore, did not value his Church position except for the money. Besides, his action had brought him wide acclaim from the people. He was immediately elected by the National Assembly to serve on the Committee of Finance, the committee charged with framing the constitution and the Committee on Education. And so he was making a transition from the ecclesiastical world to the civil. Given enough time, he was certain, he would be able to exchange his position of bishop for some high civil post which would bring him much more money. He had his eyes fixed on becoming Minister of Finance in the new government he was helping to create!

Talleyrand's contributions to all three committees were extremely valuable. He displayed great brilliance in statecraft, being a person of vision and daring. His work for the Committee on Education deserves particular notice, because the work he had done years before, investigating education for the Assembly of the Clergy, now bore fruit.

Education of the masses was close to Talleyrand's heart, and he worked hard on a long 200-page report which he gave to his committee. In it he argued that education must be taken from the hands of the Church and placed in the hands of the government and that it must be universal and compulsory. He said that tyranny had long been nourished by

ignorance, and since the new constitutional government being formed would rest on the consent of the people, the
people must be enlightened in order to understand the work-
ings of their government and contribute to its proper func-
tioning.

The measures which Talleyrand proposed for a centralized
educational system for France were not finally put into effect
until years later when Napoleon came into power. But the
work was originally done for the National Assembly. And
education in France to this very day owes a debt to the brilliance and vision of Talleyrand.

At this point in history, there were other contributions
Talleyrand made to the Revolution.

The system of weights and measures used in France was
antiquated, dating back to medieval times. Talleyrand
worked with several other members of the National Assembly
on a new and logical system, which in time became known
as the metric system and which is used today in every civilized
country in the world. We, in the United States, primarily use
the English system of weights and measures, but in certain
fields such as science and engineering we, too, use the metric
system.

Then there was the issue of paper money. It was Talleyrand who had the vision to warn the Assembly on the dangers of issuing paper money. He pointed out that paper
money is good only so long as it is backed by tangible securi-
ties such as silver, gold or land and only so long as the people
have confidence in their government. This simple principle is
universally accepted today, but at the time of the French
Revolution there were very few who understood it.

And one thing more. Talleyrand spoke out in defense of
the Portuguese Jews, who had settled in France after escaping

persecution in their native land. The monarchy had granted these Jews certain rights which had been inadvertently swept away by the Revolution along with all other rights and privileges granted to special groups by the King. Talleyrand now asked that the National Assembly reinstate these rights to the Portuguese Jews and allow them to continue to live in France enjoying tolerance and peace.

Talleyrand wanted to become the King's Minister of Finance in the new government. He had worked hard at the National Assembly and distinguished himself to a degree which warranted his receiving the appointment. However, his hopes were suddenly shattered when the Assembly voted that no member of the Assembly could serve as a Minister to the King during his term in the Assembly or for two years after.

It was a terrible disappointment. It meant that his whole future was blocked; having betrayed the Church he could not hope for an advancement to cardinal, and having served in the Assembly he now could not become a Minister of State.

However, the Assembly valued Talleyrand very highly and by a large majority it elected him President for the coming term.

Talleyrand was very pleased with this honor, which was voted in February of 1790. However, in May of the same year the relations between Church and State became so strained that his position as President of the Assembly and Bishop of Autun became embarrassing. The Church was so open in its opposition to the National Assembly and its attempt to bring a semblance of democracy to the French monarchy that the Assembly felt forced to assert its power. It, therefore, passed a bill nationalizing the Church by providing that all priests and bishops must henceforth be elected by civil authorities and by demanding that all members of the clergy, from the lowest to the highest, swear allegiance to the Constitution.

The Pope at once protested. In obedience to Rome all of the bishops serving at the National Assembly resigned—all except one. Talleyrand remained.

His estrangement from the Church was becoming more and more pronounced each day. When it was decided to hold a great celebration on the fourteenth of July, 1790, to commemorate the first anniversary of the storming of the Bastille, his ties to the Church were strained almost to the breaking point.

The celebration known as the Fête de la Fédération was held on the Champs de Mars, a great parade ground which once existed where the Eiffel Tower now stands. The Bishop of Autun celebrated the mass at this great public function of the Revolution before an altar erected in the center of the field.

In the presence of 300,000 enthusiastic supporters of Liberty, Equality, Fraternity, in the presence of the King and Queen and Lafayette, hero of the American Revolution and Commander of the National Guard, or People's Army, the Bishop of Autun in his most magnificent vestments blessed the flags of the regiments and conducted the holy services.

The climax of this celebration of the Revolution was the taking of the oath to the new Constitution. Lafayette was the first to approach the altar and repeat the words of the oath while resting the point of his sword on the altar table. Then in a united voice, the King and the people swore undying allegiance.

The ceremonies over and his work accomplished, Talleyrand left the Champs de Mars and, removing his vestments, hurried to the nearest gambling house where he engaged in such desperate playing that in a few hours he had broken the bank!

With his pockets bulging with bank notes he then dined at the home of an aristocratic lady, one of his most devoted friends. After dinner he left her to visit another gambling house where he again won vast sums. He returned late in the evening to show her his winnings. This time his hat was filled with bank notes!

Since Rome was vehemently opposed to the nationalization of the Church in France, many of the French clergy openly denounced the new government. And so the Assembly now insisted that all Churchmen—cardinals, bishops, priests, monks—take an oath of allegiance to the civil constitution or resign.

Talleyrand was, of course, one of the first to swear allegiance. However, a few weeks later he gave up his high post as bishop. He did it for personal reasons. The electors of Paris chose him as one of the administrators of the city, and wishing to devote himself wholeheartedly to his new duties, he sent the King his resignation as Bishop of Autun.

Talleyrand had at last shed his vestments but strangely enough he was not yet to be free of religious duties. This time it was the government that asked him to perform his holy rites. Since several bishops had resigned rather than swear allegiance to the State, new bishops had to be consecrated to take their places and the State needed a Churchman to perform the services.

There were several high Churchmen who could have served the State on this occasion, but one refused to do so and the others were too little known. The State wanted a man of renown. Who, they argued, could better fill the role than

Talleyrand, who had served so well at the National Assembly and had conducted the mass at the glorious Fête de la Fédération?

Talleyrand was no longer a bishop, but having once been consecrated he retained the privilege and power to consecrate. Therefore when he was asked to perform this service he accepted. However, this was the very last time that he was able to perform a religious act; having consecrated bishops without the consent of Rome, the Pope at once declared Talleyrand suspended and excommunicated and condemned to eternal damnation.

Talleyrand took his excommunication very lightly. He flippantly wrote a friend, "You know the news of my excommunication. Come and console me and dine with me. Everyone is going to refuse me bread and water, so this evening we shall have only jellied meats and chilled wine." However, some of his friends rebuked him, and his entire family disowned him, including his mother and his Uncle Alexander, Archbishop of Rheims, who had refused to take the oath and had migrated to England.

Talleyrand's mother was so distressed at the realization of the terrible mistake she had made in forcing her son to become a priest that she spent the rest of her life praying God to forgive her for the shame she had brought upon the Church.

4.

France in Chaos

❧

Talleyrand had deep faith in constitutional monarchy as a form of government. He was an aristocrat and believed in kings. He did not believe in the democratic form of government which the American colonies had established and which the extreme left or Jacobins in the National Assembly favored. And he now became deeply disturbed by the path the Revolution was taking. He was afraid that the Jacobins were going to win out and that the King was going to be completely overthrown. He sensed that disaster was close at hand.

In June of 1791, the King and Queen led on by some misguided aristocrats escaped from Paris hoping to reach eastern France where the army was still stanchly Royalist and from where the King hoped to launch a counterrevolution. Heavily disguised and accompanied by their children, they had traveled by lumbering coach throughout the dark night. However, when they reached the town of Varennes, close to the Belgian border, they were discovered and brought back to Paris. Louis was made to sign the Constitution, which was finally ready and which because of the influence of the left and extreme left, or Girondists and Jacobins, in the Assembly, reduced him to a mere figurehead. This Constitution included a Bill of Rights and provided for a legislative body called the Convention to be elected by the people.

The attempted escape had completely ruined the King's position with his people. From the day of his capture he was looked upon by all as a traitor. Talleyrand, along with the other members of the Center, feared that he might be forced to abdicate.

As if this was not distressing enough to Talleyrand, believing as he did in constitutional monarchy, there was something that worried him even more. Both the Girondists and the Jacobins wanted the Convention to declare war on every king in Europe! They felt that all the oppressed peoples of the Continent, not just the French, should enjoy Liberty, Equality, Fraternity. They were also casting a greedy eye on Belgium. They felt that France's natural border on the north and east lay at the Rhine. Besides, victories abroad would help to silence opposition at home. To eradicate these threats before they became realities and to stamp out democracy within France, Europe began to arm.

Talleyrand, who had supported the Revolution so ardently, now began to lose his enthusiasm. Still he was not able to abandon France and flee like so many other aristocrats. He loved France and did not want to desert her. He loved intrigue and politics. Yet to stay in Paris was becoming very uncomfortable, even dangerous.

To solve his dilemma he decided, in the opening weeks of the year 1792, to go to England on government business. He truly and rightly believed that it was becoming more and more essential every day to win England's friendship and neutrality. If the armies of the Revolution invaded Belgium, then certainly it was important to keep England neutral. If the armies of Europe invaded France, then, too, it was most necessary to have England's friendship. And in England one could buy horses, and the French army was at that time in dire need of horses.

With his connections in the Revolutionary government Talleyrand had little difficulty in gaining permission to cross the Channel to explore the possibility of an alliance. There was only one difficulty. His mission to England had to be unofficial because of that edict which prohibited former members of the National Assembly from holding high government offices for a period of two years. However, he was armed with all sorts of important letters. He had introductions to many members of the British government, including Prime Minister Pitt, and Louis XVI had given him a letter to King George III.

Talleyrand crossed the Channel in the most hopeful mood. He was sure that he would be welcomed to the land he so much admired, but wherever he went he was met with hostility. He was known to be an enthusiastic supporter of the Revolution, an excommunicated bishop and a desperate gambler. Besides, the French Revolution was very unpopular in England.

England's young Prime Minister Pitt, received Talleyrand stiffly. He listened but said little, as did the Secretary of Foreign Affairs. King George III was not any friendlier. He received Talleyrand but was barely civil and the Queen showed her displeasure by turning her back on Talleyrand.

His mission to England was a dismal failure, and so in March he returned to France. But within a very few weeks he was heading back again to London. The Girondists and Jacobins having won control of the Convention, France had declared war on Austria, and Prussia was on the verge of becoming involved. Talleyrand wanted desperately to try once more to win a guarantee of England's neutrality, but again he was disappointed.

England agreed to remain neutral for the time being, but she would not align herself with France as Talleyrand wanted. In June of this same year, when a mob of Girondists and Jacobins invaded the Tuileries, slaughtered the Swiss Guard, 950 strong, and forced Louis XVI to don the red cap of the Revolution and then imprisoned him and the royal family, even the most levelheaded and liberal Englishmen began to speak of joining with Austria and Prussia in war against France.

Talleyrand saw the last chances for the establishment of a constitutional monarchy in France and an accord between England and France being destroyed. He hurried back to Paris to try to save the situation if he possibly could.

Deploring the indignity which had been perpetrated against the King and the royal family, he managed to have the city council, or Commune, suspend the mayor of Paris, who was responsible for the night raid on the Tuileries. However, the Convention immediately reinstated him.

Talleyrand now felt that France was on the brink of a period of violence. He also realized that he had powerful enemies in the government and that he must leave France, but he did not want to escape through the underground like all the other émigrés. He had no wish to burn his bridges behind him; he wanted to be able to return after the Girondists and Jacobins had spent their fury. He wanted to leave in an accredited manner so that he could someday return and again serve the government. And so he decided to appeal directly to Danton, the leader of the Jacobins and new Minister of Justice.

He said that now more than ever before, with internal affairs in such a desperate turmoil and with Austrian and Prussian armies crossing the borders, France needed to win England's friendship and support, and he proposed to return to London and try again. "My real aim," he later said, "was to leave France, where it seemed useless, even dangerous for me to remain."

Danton could see that Talleyrand's idea for an alliance with England was correct. But since as a former member of the National Assembly Talleyrand still could not serve the government in any major capacity, it had to be an unofficial trip. Danton, apologized; the best he could do was to provide him with a passport.

This was exactly what Talleyrand wanted! And it was none too soon, for suddenly the violence which he sensed would come erupted. The following day there began a ghastly slaughter all over France, known in history as the September Massacres. Gangs of assassins under orders from the Jacobins, who were gaining control of the government and wanted to eradicate all opposition by terrorizing the people, entered prisons and roamed the streets butchering everyone, but especially aristocrats and priests who had raised their voices against the Revolution. The massacre lasted four days. In Paris alone, thousands were killed in cold blood without trial and without mercy.

Talleyrand was, of course, in danger; he was an aristocrat and had once belonged to the Church, and although he had worked diligently for the Revolution, he had always opposed the Girondists and Jacobins with their Republican ideas. He did not dare leave the city, for fear of attracting attention. He waited anxiously day after day. Finally, a full week later when things quieted down, he started out for England once again.

Talleyrand was now an émigré, separated from the only thing to which he was devoted, France. However, he was not doomed to live in loneliness and among strangers because England was pleased to provide a refuge for those French aristocrats who had abandoned their country in that troubled time. Arriving in London for the third time that year, he found a number of friends. Among them was Madame de Staël, the only child of the well-known banker, Necker, who had once served Louis XVI as Minister of Finance and who had proposed the Estates General, which had opened the political door to Talleyrand.

Madame de Staël, who was married to the Swedish Ambassador to the Court of Louis XVI, was undoubtedly the most brilliant and charming of all Frenchwomen. She had ruled over the most brilliant salon in Paris, the center of literary and political discussion. She was a writer—considered by some today to be the greatest of all French female writers—and her intelligence, enthusiasm and passion for life gave her an irresistible personality. Besides, she was extremely loyal to her friends, saving many from political pitfalls and the blade of the guillotine.

Talleyrand had escaped from France just in time, because shortly after he left, the Jacobins won complete control of the Convention and leadership was wrested from Danton by an extremely ruthless man named Robespierre. The Jacobins' sole purpose now was to get rid of the King.

They began in September by abolishing all royalty. In December they brought the King to trial for treason. He was found guilty on January 20, 1793, and the next day was driven through the streets in a carriage to the Place de la Revolution, now the Place de la Concorde, and beheaded on the guillotine.

The King was dead and his little son, who had automatically become Louis XVII, mysteriously disappeared, but the Jacobins were not yet satisfied. They now instituted a persecution of everyone suspected of having intrigued with Louis. The Queen was one of the first to be tried and beheaded, but there were many others. An iron box, containing letters of advice to the King from his friends and certain men in public life, had been found in the Tuileries, and all these people were ordered arrested and tried. They all lost their heads.

Talleyrand was the writer of several of these letters, but since he was in England he was safe. However, on March 28 his name was added by the Jacobins to a list which they had compiled of *Enemies of the Revolution,* and it was decreed that if ever he set foot on French soil he was to be guillotined.

The winter of 1792–1793 was eventful indeed, for it witnessed not only the rise of Robespierre, the execution of the King and the beginning of the Reign of Terror, but also the invasion of France by Prussian and Austrian troops and England's abandonment of neutrality. England now joined with the enemies of France, threatening to send military aid to help put an end to the Revolution. Talleyrand's dream of an alliance between France and England was shattered.

However, he did not give up. He was convinced that the Jacobins would eventually be replaced by saner men. Then he would return to France and to his plan for strong ties with England. Yes, he would be patient; from London he would watch the political scene in Paris, and at the right moment he would return.

But suddenly in January, 1794, without previous warning,

the British government asked him to leave England. He was accused of being an enemy alien—an undesirable.

Where could he go? Every country on the Continent was pitted against France, and with his record as a revolutionary, he would most certainly be unwelcome. There was only one country that would give him refuge, the United States. Americans understood revolutionists. Besides, they liked the French because of the help France had given them in their Revolution against the British. He booked passage on a vessel that was sailing from London for America in the first week of March.

5.

America

⚜

Talleyrand spent thirty-eight monotonous days crossing the Atlantic. Then sailing into the mouth of the Delaware River, his vessel docked at Philadelphia, which was at that time serving as temporary capital of the United States. The year was 1794 and George Washington was just beginning to serve his second term as President of the United States.

Back in 1789 when the Bastille was besieged by the mob, Washington had only been in office a few months, and he, like all other Americans, had hailed the event as the dawn of a new era. Lafayette, his cherished friend, had sent him the great iron key of the demolished prison and Washington had accepted the gift as a "token of victory gained by liberty." This famous key may be seen today in Mount Vernon.

However, America's approval of the French Revolution did not last very long, for it was soon realized that what was happening in France was very different from what had happened in America. When the Jacobins came into power and the Reign of Terror cast its blood-red shadow over France, American enthusiasm for the French Revolution quickly turned to revulsion.

Thomas Jefferson, a true son of liberty and the architect of American democracy, was serving President Washington as Secretary of State; and when he saw how things were going in France, he proposed that Washington issue a proclamation of neutrality. This Washington did.

Talleyrand landed in America in a climate that was not as friendly as he had hoped it might be. He was looked upon with suspicion. Some even believed that he had come to America as an agent of the Jacobins! The French Ambassador to the United States said, "If Talleyrand is received at the President's Palace, I will never set foot in it again; you must choose between an émigré and me."

Washington, who was by nature most considerate and courteous, did not dare entertain Talleyrand. He could not as President disregard the French Ambassador's wishes and endanger United States relations with a friendly nation. Besides, he had just declared the United States neutral and was anxious to keep it so.

Before leaving London, Talleyrand had said that "America is a country that should be seen," and so he did not spend all his time in Philadelphia but went on a number of trips to New York, Albany and Boston. He even journeyed through the New England States. But he did not like what he saw.

He did not like American cooking. He thought the climate was terrible—too cold in winter, too hot in summer. He was surprised to find that the frontier started only fifty miles west of Philadelphia and that many pioneering crudities existed even closer to the city. He felt that Americans lacked culture and were too preoccupied with commerce and the making of money. He himself was passionately fond of money, but he always hid his interest under an air of refined disdain;

Americans he felt showed their interest too openly and crudely! And as for American cities . . .

The United States was at that time made up of only thirteen states with a total population of four million, and by the standards of the day, Philadelphia was considered a big city. It had 80,000 inhabitants. To Talleyrand, accustomed to the great cathedrals, avenues, parks, government buildings and magnificent palaces and homes of Paris and London, it seemed very quaint indeed, with its quiet little streets lined on both sides with simple red brick houses.

He was very lonely. He longed for his native land, his friends, the comforts of his old life. He was in financial straits and was forced to live in one small room overlooking an alley. Yet, he made the best of his lot. He still believed that France would eventually return to sanity and that he would then be able to go home. Reports from France indicated that even the Jacobins were growing tired of so much brutality. Too many innocent heads had fallen into the executioner's basket. Rumors indicated that the French had had their fill of the Terror and were casting about for more reasonable leaders. It was said that in some quarters the whisper of "Peace" could be heard. Talleyrand was encouraged, and he decided that while waiting, he would try to engage in some commercial ventures.

To Madame de Staël he wrote, "Reason tells me that I must repair my fortunes a bit in order to avoid continual dependence." While he criticized Americans for their absorption in money matters, he was quick to seize upon some of the many fine opportunities for making money which were constantly cropping up in the rapidly growing United States. From Boston he again wrote to his friend Madame de Staël about money, this time asking her help. "There are more chances to remake one's fortune here than in any other place," he said. He suggested that she persuade her banker father to send merchandise to America which he would undertake to sell. "In a short time one can make a great deal of money," he assured her.

Shortly after this letter he enlarged upon his plan. He suggested sending a ship laden with American produce to India. The merchants of Philadelphia, he felt, would be very eager to underwrite such a venture and he envisioned enormous profits. And he was right. Before long he had accumulated 50,000 francs, the equivalent of $10,000 in our money with a purchasing power many, many times what it would have been today.

The dream of wealth was ever with him, and he would probably have become very rich in America had he remained, but suddenly the political change for which he had been waiting occurred in France and so all his plans were changed.

The news of Robespierre's fall reached Talleyrand one day in 1794 while he was visiting General Schuyler at his mansion in Albany, New York.

Talleyrand had left his host for a few hours to visit some friends in nearby Troy. On his return he found the General waiting for him on the porch, waving his hands in frantic excitement.

"Come, come quickly! There is great news from France," he cried.

The post had brought the latest dispatches telling of a great upheaval. The Reign of Terror had ended. Robespierre had been arrested and put to death under the blade of the very guillotine to which he had condemned so many and a new Constitution had been adopted. The French government was now called the Directory and consisted of a board of five Directors and a Congress, or Convention, divided into an Upper and Lower House called the Council of Ancients and the Council of Five Hundred.

Talleyrand's return to France was now possible. First, however, he would have to have his name removed from the list of *Enemies of the Revolution*. And so again he appealed to his devoted friend Madame de Staël, who had herself only recently returned to Paris, where her husband, the Swedish Ambassador, had reopened his embassy.

"I shall die," Talleyrand wrote, "if I remain here another year."

He knew that the beautiful and brilliant Madame de Staël knew everyone of importance in Paris. He also knew that she had tact and understood how to negotiate behind the scenes. He felt certain that she would do him this favor, which she did.

For her important task Madame de Staël enlisted the services of Marie-Joseph Chénier, one of the best orators in the new Convention. To gain his full sympathy she first appealed to his emotions, giving him a pitiful picture of what it meant to be an exile. She then aroused his sense of justice. She said that Talleyrand was a victim of circumstances. She said that he had always been loyal to France and the Revolution. Had he not taken a courageous stand in the Assembly against his own order, the Clergy? Was it not he who had laid the great wealth of the Church at the feet of the People? Was he not the statesman who had tried to keep England neutral?

Chénier was impressed. A few days later he rose in the Convention to stir his hearers with the great services that "Talleyrand-Périgord, ex-Bishop of Autun, had rendered the National Assembly." He called him "one of the founders of liberty." He said that Talleyrand had gone to England on a mission for the government and that it was Danton himself who had given him his passport. To prove this he quoted from one of Talleyrand's letters to Danton written from London.

Chénier then spoke of Talleyrand's exile in America. "It was in the heart of a Republic, in the country of Benjamin Franklin, that he contemplated the impressive spectacle of a free people, awaiting the time when France should possess judges and not assassins, a Republic and not an Anarchy."

He ended his fiery speech with an appeal to permit Talleyrand to return to France. "I claim him in the name of his many services. I claim him in the name of national equity. I claim him in the name of the Republic to which his talents may be of service and in the name of the hatred you bear to émigrés of whom he would be the victim, like yourselves, if cowards could triumph."

The entire Convention was moved by Chénier's eloquence. It immediately voted to erase Talleyrand's name from the hateful list of *Enemies of the Revolution* and granted him permission to return to France.

Talleyrand received the official notice of his pardon in November, 1795, but he did not board ship at once for France. He had two reasons for waiting. He did not want to cross the Atlantic during the stormy winter months and he wanted to wait and see if the new French government would endure. He always believed, "Time will do its work," and time was now needed to see whether the new government would be able to meet the many problems it had inherited: a frightened and hungry people, an empty treasury, vast armies in the field and greatly extended boundaries, for surprising as it may seem, the French Revolutionary Army had won on all fronts. It had overwhelmed the Piedmontese and captured

Savoy and Nice in the south. It had penetrated the German states as far as Frankfurt and the Rhine, capturing Mainz. And to the north it had overrun Belgium, capturing Antwerp.

So Talleyrand decided to wait. In fact, he waited until June, almost seven months after receiving his pardon from the Directory, before sailing for home. To avoid England, which was at war with France, he booked passage on a Danish vessel going to Hamburg. It was not, in fact, until September that he finally returned to Paris, ending four long years of exile.

Talleyrand was now forty-two years old. Was it possible at this age for him to begin anew? Ambition was still aflame within him and his confidence in himself had not diminished. He was ready and eager to re-enter the political scene.

While waiting those long months in Philadelphia, he had not been idle. He had been informing himself through letters and periodicals on conditions in France and on the background of the men who made up the Directory. He had done even more than that. He had decided what role he wanted to play in the new government. He had reached the decision that since the Directory had no experienced diplomatic statesman, no one who really understood the complex problems which existed between the countries of Europe, he would serve France in that field.

Yes, he had made up his mind. He would serve the Directory as its Minister of Foreign Affairs!

6.

Foreign Affairs and Fortune

⚜

Paris was a city transformed. During the four years of Talley-rand's absence, four years of violence and terror, great changes had occurred. The grandeur of aristocratic life, the palaces, the great parties, the silk clothes and powdered hair, the feather headdresses, the furs, the jewels, the coaches, all were gone. The broad paved boulevards were now unpaved rivers of mud. The finest homes were dilapidated, monuments ruined, churches plundered and forsaken.

But the people were gayer. Those who had survived the guillotine were now dancing. They had lived through untold horrors, and now it was time to celebrate their release from tyranny. Fear, suspicion and gloom gave way to laughter, gaiety and frenzied revelry.

With this change of mood had come a drastic change in fashions. Women dressed in flowing muslin dresses. Their legs were bare. They wore sandals and rings on their toes and their hair was cut short and curled in Roman style. Men wrapped enormous cravats about their necks, covering their chins. Hats were pulled down to the eyebrows. Coats were loose and shapeless.

Four years had, indeed, brought about great changes, but Talleyrand did not waste his time mourning for the past. He always had the wisdom to accept things as they were, and so he quickly adjusted to the new ways and concentrated on renewing old friendships, making new ones and laying plans for resuming his political career. It was not long before he found the opportunity he was seeking.

Some years before, when he was in the National Assembly and had presented his report on public education, he had proposed that a National Institute be established to which the best scientists, scholars and writers of France would be elected. During his exile this National Institute had become a reality. As soon as the Directory had come into power and his name had been removed from the lists of *Enemies of the Revolution,* and while he was still in America, he had been elected a member of the division of political science. Now that he was back in Paris, he received an invitation to deliver a lecture to the distinguished members of the Institute. This was the chance for which he had been waiting; at one stroke he would bring his name once more to the attention of the public and establish himself as an authority in the field of foreign affairs.

He chose his subject carefully. Interest in the young Republic across the Atlantic was very keen in France; he was the only Frenchman then in Paris well informed on the United States. The subject of his lecture was, "The Commercial Relations between the United States and England."

Talleyrand was correct. Interest in America was so great that his lecture was very well attended. While, in accordance with his subject, he spent much time discussing commerce, he also spoke of things that went beyond trade and money matters, things which displayed his keen powers of observation and insight.

During his discourse he gave the members of the Institute a general description of the United States, the character of its people, their religious freedom, their love of liberty and their respect for law. He also spoke of their sentiment for France. However, he reminded his audience of the fact that Americans were traditionally, emotionally and socially quite like the English; that their language, their laws, their system of education and other institutions had come from England and that it was therefore to England that America's future would be bound. He concluded that England and the United States would be economically dependent upon each other even though their political ties had been broken. He went further. He implied that, in spite of America's gratitude to France for the help she had given during the American Revolution, France could not count on increased trade with the United States. Neither could she expect political cooperation.

Talleyrand had not misjudged. The members of the Institute were, of course, all highly intelligent and distinguished in their fields, and they immediately recognized that Talleyrand possessed a rare and penetrating critical faculty. They recognized too that he had just presented facts to them which very few people at that time understood, facts which were important to the future of France, in shaping her policy with England and the United States. They were impressed. Going their separate ways, they spoke of Talleyrand everywhere in the most glowing terms.

Having succeeded in bringing his name once more to the attention of the public, Talleyrand now wanted to impress the Directors of the government with his abilities. Having carefully studied the background of each, he decided to con-

centrate his efforts on Barras, the only man who like himself
came from the upper classes.

Barras was a former Viscount who had played the chief role
in overthrowing Robespierre and crushing the terrible Reign
of Terror. It was he who, between the fall of Robespierre and
the establishment of the Directory, had acted as head of the
French government with the powers of a dictator. It was he,
also, who had defied a mob crying for the restoration of the
monarchy and threatening the building where the Convention was meeting to formulate the Directory. He had put a
twenty-six-year-old Brigadier General named Napoleon Bonaparte in command of troops and told him to disperse the
crowd. The young officer had displayed extreme daring; he
had aimed his cannons into the mob. One "whiff of grapeshot" had been enough; one hundred had fallen dead and
the government had been saved.

It was clear to Talleyrand that Barras was the most important member of the Directory. The other four were either
lawyers or former captains of Revolutionary forces. Barras
alone had the qualities of a leader. He was the one to be
cultivated, and since Madame de Staël liked nothing better
than to engage in just such a campaign, Talleyrand asked her
to work in his behalf.

Madame de Staël was delighted with her assignment, and
she at once laid siege to Barras with subtle maneuvers, femi-
nine charm, intrigue and eloquence. She created reasons for
making frequent visits to his office, and on these visits she
sang the praises of Talleyrand. She spoke of his talents at
persuasion, his rare gifts for reasoning, his wisdom, his foresight, his social charm. She pointed out that there was no one
in the present French government who possessed a knowledge
of kings, princes and foreign ministers. And she said that

there was no one who knew better than Talleyrand how to deal with such dignitaries and extract the best results from difficult situations.

When the ground was properly prepared she then arranged for Barras and Talleyrand to meet. A few days later she was able to report to Talleyrand that her campaign had been completely successful; Barras had decided that Talleyrand was just the man the Directory needed. He was to be Minister of Foreign Affairs.

Talleyrand was at home with a friend when the good news reached him, and this man has left a record of Talleyrand's reaction. The friend reports that Talleyrand was so overjoyed that for a few moments he completely lost his composure and embraced him and the gentleman who had brought the message. Then deciding to drive over to thank Barras in person, he insisted that they both come with him. In the carriage his joy overflowed and he repeated several times, "I'm now Minister of Foreign Affairs! Minister of Foreign Affairs! I'll make an immense fortune out of it; a truly immense fortune!"

Talleyrand was officially named Minister of Foreign Affairs on July 18, 1797, and one of the first acts he performed displayed his uncanny power for seeing into the future. The first letter he wrote after taking office was addressed to that young military officer who had fired into the Parisian mob and who was now concluding a victorious campaign in Italy. Without authorization from the Directory, he wrote a letter to Napoleon Bonaparte.

Talleyrand had never met Napoleon, but that did not deter him. He had followed the young man's progress during the Italian campaign and had informed himself about his background and training and he had decided that the young

General was a man worth cultivating. He sensed that Napoleon was a man with a future and he felt that they could be useful to each other.

"I have the honor to inform you, General," he wrote, "that the executive Directory has appointed me Minister of Foreign Affairs." Then with much grace he went on to say that the glory of Napoleon's victories would be of invaluable help to him in foreign negotiations. "The very name Bonaparte will help overcome all difficulties."

It was a most friendly letter and ended with these flattering words, "There is a quality of greatness and stability that you give to everything you do."

Having taken the first step in winning Napoleon's friendship, Talleyrand now settled down to his duties as Foreign Minister and to the very pleasing task of building that "immense fortune" he coveted so dearly.

The Revolution had changed everything in France—laws, ancient customs, education, religion, clothing—everything except corruption. That alone survived unchanged. And so Talleyrand, like most other government officials, felt perfectly free to demand bribes for everything he did, and within a few weeks he had one million livres in his pocket. It represented his share of an eight-million-livre bribe which he had extracted from Portugal in exchange for certain concessions. Barras had received three million of the eight million and the four other Directors, like Talleyrand, had each received one million!

As Minister of Foreign Affairs, Talleyrand controlled the fate of many countries. And he felt that if his knowledge and talents could secure benefits for foreign lands without in any way hurting France, he was entitled to a present. He said very openly that concessions must be paid for. Like most other French diplomats of the time, Talleyrand considered the thing we call "extortion" and "graft" as nothing more than a kind of "sweetness," a gracious present due for services performed and not unlike a commission paid a broker.

Trying to explain his complete lack of morality, he said, "In life one must be realistic." He had known the inconveniences of poverty when he was young and again as an exile in the United States. He said, "First and foremost, one must be rich."

Talleyrand's lack of "principles" pleased the five government Directors. They had benefited very handsomely from his corruption. But shortly after the treaty with Portugal was signed, Talleyrand led them into a very embarrassing situation with a country whose diplomats were not corrupt, the United States of America. This page of history is known as the XYZ Affair.

During the closing days of George Washington's administration, the United States signed Jay's Treaty with Great Britain; it was negotiated for the United States by Chief Justice John Jay, a former member of the Continental Congress. This treaty angered France because it not only eradicated many of the grievances which existed between Great Britain and her former colonies but actually rendered meaningless certain agreements which had existed between France and the United States. To show her displeasure France, therefore, began preying on American ships on the high seas. She seized a great number of American vessels; the sailors were beaten and imprisoned and the ships sold. Before long the loss to American merchants and shipowners reached fifty-five million dollars and public indignation in the United States mounted to a high pitch.

President John Adams, who had succeeded George Washington, denounced the conduct of France and ordered all American merchant ships to be converted into warships. However, still hoping to avoid open conflict with France, he sent a special mission to Paris consisting of Pinckney of South Carolina, Gerry of Massachusetts and John Marshall of Virginia. All three had distinguished themselves during the American Revolution. Pinckney had served General Washington as his aide-de-camp and had been a member of the Constitutional Convention. Gerry had served as a member of the first National Congress and had signed the Declaration of Independence; he was later to become Vice-President of the United States under James Monroe. John Marshall had served in Washington's army throughout the Revolution and was a member of the Virginia Executive Council. He was to distinguish himself still further as Secretary of State under Adams and as Chief Justice of the Supreme Court. It was he who raised the Supreme Court to a position of power and majesty and endowed the federal government with unity and strength by the broad scope and vision of his interpretations of the Constitution.

How would Talleyrand's "principles" fare with men of this caliber?

Marshall, Pinckney and Gerry were received by three of Talleyrand's assistants, men who were well trained in diplomatic extortion. In very refined but devious language the Frenchmen suggested that America's claim would be considered and brought to a happy termination only if the Directors of the French government and the Minister of Foreign Affairs could have something for their trouble. They suggested that $240,000 would be a suitable sum. This $240,000 could bring about the most friendly relations between France and America!

The American envoys were shocked by this outrageous demand. They left Paris at once and, reaching home, published an indignant report. For diplomatic reasons they did not reveal the real names of Talleyrand's three intermediaries; they referred to them as X, Y and Z.

The whole affair, now that it has been brought out into the open, became a scandal of the greatest importance on both sides of the Atlantic. France quickly backed down, and there were no further attacks on American merchant ships.

Talleyrand and his confederates had been soundly rebuked. France was never again to attempt such coercion with the United States. However, Talleyrand was left in a very embarrassing position. To save himself from complete disgrace, he, therefore, immediately sent the Paris press an official disavowal of X, Y and Z. He insisted that he was entirely innocent of the attempted extortion.

He had saved face and his high post as Foreign Minister, but everyone in Paris knew that he and the five Directors were involved and would have shared in the booty. The French people knew very well that X, Y and Z were not only assistants to Talleyrand in the Ministry of Foreign Affairs but also his personal friends and were associated with him in speculation, financial manipulation and extortion.

War had been averted and the United States had gained prestige on the diplomatic front, but this was not all. Talleyrand's miscalculation had an effect of far greater importance, an effect which was international in scope and which was to gain in meaning with each passing year. Three hundred American merchant ships were now armed and ready for war. These vessels constituted the beginning of the United States Navy. A new sea power had been born.

7.

The Meeting of Two Giants

❦

Ever since that day when Napoleon dispersed the mob with a "whiff of grapeshot" Talleyrand had followed his every movement with the utmost satisfaction. He had watched from afar as Napoleon assumed command of the starving and ragged French army in Italy and transformed it into a powerful fighting force. He had followed with the greatest of interest Napoleon's capture of the Kingdom of Sardinia and his victories over the Austrian-Sardinian forces at Lodi, Milan, Naples, Arcole, Rivoli and Mantua. He had been greatly impressed by Napoleon's wisdom when, after crossing the Alps to fight the Austrians and being victorious in the first encounters, he had terminated his campaign and negotiated the peace of Campo Formio. He had written him many letters in which he reiterated in different words the closing thought of his first letter, "There is a quality of greatness and stability that you give to everything you do."

Now, at last, he was to meet this remarkable young man who was fifteen years his junior. News had reached Paris that the victorious Bonaparte was on his way to the capital. Every-

one awaited his arrival. His name was on every lip. But it was
Talleyrand who was to be privileged to see him first.

Napoleon arrived at Paris on the evening of December 5
and immediately sent a message to Talleyrand asking for an
interview. He had discerned from Talleyrand's letters that
here was a man of superior mind, a man he could use. He was
extremely anxious to meet him and did not mask his eager-
ness.

Talleyrand, who was just as eager, was delighted to receive
Napoleon's note and invited the young hero to the Ministry
of Foreign Affairs, a beautiful palace on the Rue de Bac
which also served as his home, at eleven o'clock the following
morning.

Beholding Napoleon for the first time, Talleyrand fell
under his hypnotic spell. He later recorded, "Bonaparte
seemed to me to have a charming face. Twenty victories go so
well with youth, with a fine look and with a sort of exhaus-
tion."

Talleyrand was also pleased to hear Napoleon say that he
had enjoyed corresponding with someone who was "different
from the Directors."

Indeed, they were both pleased with each other. They left
the room arm in arm, going into an adjoining sitting room
where fifty of Talleyrand's friends were waiting to meet the
twenty-eight-year-old conqueror. They crowded around Napoleon showering him with words of praise. Madame de Staël,
who was among them, kneeled humbly at his feet. It was only
then, when the excitement began to subside, that Napoleon
paid his respects to the five Directors.

Five days later Napoleon was officially received by the
Directory. But he did not go alone. Talleyrand called for
him in his private carriage and rode with him across Paris to

the Luxembourg through the wildly cheering crowds. It was also Talleyrand who officially introduced the new hero of France to the Directory and all those other notables who had gathered for this joyous occasion.

Talleyrand had "captured" Napoleon with flattery and was now building a public image of himself as Napoleon's closest friend and adviser. He was in control and he was determined to use every moment to advantage. Therefore, looking out over the audience and noticing certain uneasy faces, which seemed to be asking, "Is this rising star a new Caesar?" he quickly tried to dispel suspicion. He assured the audience that Napoleon, while a victorious general, was a man of peace and completely lacking in personal ambition. According to Talleyrand, Napoleon was in fact a retiring scholar! "I feel that we shall have to beg him to come away from the sweetness of his studious retreat . . ." he said.

Napoleon now rose to speak. However, he had very little to say. He uttered only five sentences and what he said was delivered in a very blunt and jerky manner. But this did not trouble Talleyrand. As Napoleon voiced his fifth and last sentence, "When the happiness of the French people is founded on the best organic laws . . ." Talleyrand leaned forward and whispered to a friend, "The future stands there."

Talleyrand felt that the future belonged to Napoleon. He had just said so. However, he had not whispered everything he felt to his friend. He had not revealed that he believed the future belonged to both of them—Napoleon and Talleyrand.

Two giants had found each other. Together they planned to dominate the Directory. However, their first joint effort met with almost complete defeat.

The Directory held the same view that the Revolutionary government had always held, which was that every country in

Europe must cast off its king and adopt a republican form of government like that which France had established. If any country refused to do this, French armies should invade this country and force it to adopt democracy. In order to further this plan the Directory wanted to invade England, which had been using her military might to help protect Europe against French aggression. If England were vanquished, all Europe would be forced to do as France dictated.

Intoxicated with his victories in Italy, Napoleon liked the idea of attacking England. But after carefully weighing every aspect of such an invasion, he decided it was too dangerous to undertake without long and careful preparations. He feared a disaster and advised postponing the invasion of England until some other time. For the time being he proposed harrying England by threatening India. He suggested that if France conquered Egypt, which was then under Turkish domination, England's attention would be drawn away from Europe and directed toward the Orient. While she was thus occupied abroad, France could have her way in Europe.

Talleyrand immediately supported Napoleon's plan. He did not approve of France's desire to force democracy upon the rest of Europe. He felt that France should contain her ideals within her own boundaries and make friends with her neighbors, especially England. He still dreamed of an alliance between France and England, an alliance which would by sheer strength guarantee the peace of Europe. So he supported Napoleon's proposal for waging war outside of Europe with all his might, becoming so enthusiastic that he began speaking of turning the Mediterranean into a "French Sea."

The Directory soon became infected by his enthusiasm. Before long it had granted Napoleon and Talleyrand permission to work together to prepare an expeditionary force for invading Egypt.

Thus it was that Napoleon's Egyptian campaign was born. Thus it was that Napoleon and his forces set out from Toulon with the greatest of hopes. However, from the moment Napoleon and his troops set foot upon Egyptian soil he was faced with failure. The good fortune he had thus far enjoyed seemed to forsake him.

Napoleon's first reversal struck almost immediately, unleashing a whole series of threats to European peace. The French navy that had brought his forces to Egypt was captured and completely destroyed by Nelson on its return journey to Toulon. This meant that he and his men were now cut off from supplies and must win with what arms they had or perish.

The effect of this on the morale of Napoleon's troops was, of course, devastating, and so his forces lost all the opening encounters in which they engaged. Encouraged by Napoleon's reverses and angered by the invasion of Egypt, Turkey now declared war on France. This gave courage to some of the republics which Napoleon had established in Italy after his conquest of that land, and they revolted against French domination. Added to all this, Austria and Russia now rallied the smaller countries of Europe to join with them in making war on France: now, they said, was the golden moment to strike Revolutionary France and eradicate forever the scourge of Republicanism.

With these dark clouds of disaster gathering so rapidly around her, France was once more shaken by unrest. The Directory was openly criticized. Talleyrand, who was, of course, partly responsible for the situation, realized that it would soon fall. He gave it a few months at the most.

What should he do? He had no intention of going down
with the government. To do so would discredit him and
render him ineligible for a post in the next government, so
he decided to abandon the sinking ship. He must save himself
at all cost because he did not want to disappear from the
political scene. He wanted to amass a fortune—an immense
fortune—and so creating certain pretexts, he asked to be relieved of his duties as Minister of Foreign Affairs.

His resignation was accepted July 20, 1798. He was now
free. And as he predicted, the Directory soon fell. But it did
not fall of its own accord; strangely enough Talleyrand was
one of those instrumental in bringing about its sorry end.

Napoleon thrived on victories but withered when faced
with defeat. Being thwarted on every side, he longed to leave
the scorching deserts of Egypt and return to the European
terrain which he understood and where he had waged such
successful campaigns. Besides, news of the troubles in Europe
had reached him in every mail. Some of the letters were
from Talleyrand, and he had become possessed with a burning desire to play a part in these disturbing affairs. He longed
to restore order in Italy and lead the French armies to victory
against the Austrians and Russians. If the Directory would
only make him Commander-in-Chief of the French Army. . . !
He had also come to the conclusion that the Directory must
be strengthened. He felt it was too weak. It was ineffectual.
Perhaps he should become one of the five Directors. However, he could not return to France as a completely defeated
soldier; he had to wait until he had won some sort of victory.
So he tried to march his disease-ridden and half-starving men
into Syria, searching for glory but without success.

Returning to Egypt his plight grew more desperate each
day. Because he could not spare the food, he shot his prison-

ers. Then suddenly and miraculously his luck changed. He won a victory over a Turkish force far superior to his in numbers. This was the moment for which he had been waiting. Abandoning his army in this foreign land without proper supplies and food, he secretly set sail for France on a merchant ship.

It was a long trip and fraught with dangers. He narrowly escaped being captured by the British who were patrolling the Mediterranean and searching all vessels. However, after forty-seven days, he finally landed safely on the southern coast of France and headed north at once for Paris.

The moment Talleyrand heard that Napoleon had landed on the coast of France and was rushing toward the capital, he guessed at his intention—Napoleon wanted to take advantage of the political unrest at home to further himself. Since Talleyrand firmly believed that Napoleon was "the future," he was more than sympathetic and was one of the first to see him when he finally reached Paris.

Napoleon greeted Talleyrand as an old and loyal friend. Even though Talleyrand was no longer part of the government, he felt that he could be of great value to him and he immediately and very frankly revealed his wishes. He said that he wanted to become a member of the Directory and also Commander-in-Chief.

Talleyrand listened carefully to everything Napoleon said and then promised his complete support. Having once pledged himself, he then entered wholeheartedly into Napoleon's scheme.

He explained to Napoleon that there were only two of the five Directors who had any real power and that they were both his personal friends. One was Barras and the other was a recently elected member named Sieyès. Barras had called on

Napoleon to disperse the crowd with a "whiff of grapeshot" and had given him command of the armies for the successful Italian campaign. He knew Napoleon and was proud of him. But Sieyès . . . Talleyrand was not certain of his views and whether or not he could be persuaded to help Napoleon. Nevertheless, Talleyrand agreed to try to win him over, a task he immediately and successfully accomplished. Since Sieyès controlled a third Director called Ducos, he automatically also gained his support. From that moment on events moved swiftly.

During the three critical weeks that followed Napoleon's return to Paris, Talleyrand worked without rest. He knew everyone. He knew their opinions and their friends. He knew who could be useful and whom to avoid. He himself never seemed to be involved. Yet, he held the strings in his hands and pulled each one at exactly the proper time, making even the most exalted men bounce around like puppets.

The result was that Napoleon's desire to become Commander-in-Chief and a Director of the government became more elaborate each day until it finally evolved as a plot to completely overthrow the Directory and place Napoleon at the head of France!

The plan was simple. The three Directors—Barras, Sieyès and Ducos—would resign simultaneously. The two remaining Directors, who were opposed to Napoleon, would be brushed aside, and the Council of Ancients would make Napoleon Commander-in-Chief. The Council of Five Hundred would then be dissolved, and the Ancients would proclaim a new government called a Consulate.

The fateful day, November 9, 1799, finally arrived and the plot began to unfold.

The Ancients ordered that both legislative bodies move to

St. Cloud just outside of Paris, claiming that a Jacobin plot to seize the government had been uncovered and that the peace of Paris was threatened. The truth was that at St. Cloud there would be very few to witness the events which were about to take place. The Ancients then placed all the troops of Paris and the surrounding territory under Napoleon's command. Barras, Sieyès and Ducos resigned as planned. The two remaining Directors were seized and placed under military "protection."

Napoleon, accompanied by four grenadiers, appeared before the Council of Five Hundred and ordered that body to dissolve without delay! He had stationed troops outside.

Violent shouts immediately rent the air. Some cried, "Outlaw!" Others shrieked, "Traitor!"

Then the unexpected happened. This was a new kind of battlefield. Napoleon lost his nerve, turned pale and nearly fainted. He had to be dragged from the hall by his grenadiers. Once outside, he quickly recovered his composure. Turning to his troops he ordered them into the hall with bayonets drawn.

The delegates scattered in terror. They rushed through the nearest doors and jumped from the windows. Only a few remained to protest against this armed intrusion. However, the soldiers soon dragged them out by force.

When it was certain that the Council of Five Hundred had been dissolved, the Ancients then completed the last act of the plan. That high body voted to place the government in the hands of three Consuls: Napoleon, Sieyès and Ducos. They were to rule jointly while a new constitution was being drawn up.

Thus was Napoleon's *coup d'état* accomplished. Thus was the Directory dissolved in a single day. The people received the news with jubilation. They were tired and disgusted with the blood, terror and changing governments through which they had lived since the Revolution had erupted ten and a half years before with the opening of the Estates General. They longed for peace and stability. They believed that freedom was now to be established on a firm basis by Napoleon, a man who was affiliated with no special political group and who had proven himself to be a most able leader and administrator during the Italian campaign.

Talleyrand, who had helped engineer Napoleon's *coup d'état* shared this opinion. He was there at St. Cloud on this historical day. He wanted to witness the dramatic events with his own eyes.

8.

Napoleon's Minister

❧

Napoleon had overthrown the Directory and been named as one of the three Consuls, but he was not satisfied. Within a very short time, acting boldly and swiftly, he elevated himself to the position of First Consul for a ten-year term and replaced Sieyès and Ducos with men of his own choice.

He was a man of decision and action. Using men from all political factions he immediately reorganized the government into such a smoothly running and efficient machine that almost all opposition disappeared. Former terrorists became quiet active councilors and administrators. Jacobins were given "bones to gnaw on." In short, everyone was given a post to satisfy his ego and was so overwhelmed with work there was no time for fomenting trouble.

Napoleon was, indeed, a man of strength and political brilliance, yet he needed help in governing France and so he chose his Ministers with utmost care. He picked only the most able to serve on his cabinet. He needed every bit of guidance these men could give him. Above all he needed Talleyrand, and he made him Minister of Foreign Affairs.

Napoleon needed him because Talleyrand was a living

source of scholarly information and knew protocol, international relations and foreign lands, including even the United States. He also needed him because, as the ex-Bishop of Autun, he knew a great deal about internal Church affairs and the political intricacies of the Vatican. He said, "Talleyrand has what is needed in negotiations: worldliness, familiarity with the courts of Europe, cleverness that keeps him from saying too much, facial immobility which reveals nothing and, finally, a great name."

Yes, Napoleon needed Talleyrand for these reasons, but he also needed him for something more personal. Napoleon had come from a poor and simple Corsican family, and he wanted passionately to be an aristocrat. He yearned for good manners, education, refined language and the elegance of breeding. He had married Josephine, whose first husband had been guillotined as an aristocrat, and she provided him with a social background and a home of distinction. But of all the men in Paris it was Talleyrand, and only Talleyrand, who represented to Napoleon "the style of Versailles." Through Talleyrand he could meet all the great princes of France, all the great princes of Europe. Through Talleyrand he could acquire that ease of manner, that pride, that craftiness and bold arrogance which were so typical of aristocrats. Through Talleyrand he could learn to be a prince. Speaking to Talleyrand one day, Napoleon summed up his feelings by saying, "I know all that you do not know; but you know all that I do not know."

Talleyrand, on the other hand, also needed Napoleon. He believed that working with him he could realize his dream of bringing stability to France and peace to Europe; together they could enforce a workable government at home and enter into an alliance with England.

His second reason for needing Napoleon was not such a noble one. It too was personal. As Napoleon's Minister of Foreign Affairs he could increase the wealth he had begun to collect under the Directory. With any luck at all, he could soon amass a great fortune, "a truly immense fortune." And to make sure that no one should thwart his plans, he immediately announced upon taking up his office that as Minister of Foreign Affairs he would collaborate with no one but the First Consul!

Talleyrand's reasons for joining Napoleon were calculated ones, but it must also be said that he truly admired the young General who had blazed his way onto the political scene, and he had genuine devotion for him. He worried about his health and his communications to him often contained such thoughts as: "I do not like your library; you spend too much time there. The ground floor is worth nothing to you. You are made for the heights." And, "Since I am bound up in your fate, I belong to you in life as well as death!"

Napoleon was the man of the hour. And to this rising star Talleyrand was now bound; he was to help steer his course. However, this was not an easy task, for their aims and methods were very different.

Napoleon sought personal glory and power and had boundless energy and a compulsive drive. He put in long hours, dictating orders and letters. He met with dozens of government officials and visitors each day. He attended an endless series of functions, reviewed his troops, inspected supplies, made plans for the Army, the Navy, for changing the laws. Nothing escaped his attention. He had an inexhaustible supply of nervous energy.

Talleyrand was just the opposite. He wanted peace for France and Europe and he loved idleness. He said that a

capacity for idleness and quiet contemplation was the best
attribute a diplomat could have. He did not even allow his
lowliest clerks to work too hard. He did not believe that hard
work accomplished very much. In defense of his theory, he
was to say in later years, "Napoleon was always thankful that
I had delayed the execution of his orders because it gave him
time to abandon resolutions which he had made too quickly."

Talleyrand had many able assistants, and he did not believe
in doing anything that one of them could do. He even
allowed them to compose important documents and treaties
for him. He would scribble one or two provisions or a se-
quence of ideas on a scrap of paper and hand it to one of
them. Later he would look over the rough draft and perhaps
change a word here, or a sentence there, and that was all.

It must be remembered, however, that he had personally
trained all his assistants in the language he liked to use for
diplomatic relations. This language was his own. When written or spoken it had a grace and special manner. And it
presented even the most drastic matters without offensive
harshness while still retaining the force of the idea he wanted
to convey.

The people of France believed that Napoleon would bring
them peace. They were wrong, as they were very soon to learn.
He was a militarist, possessed with dreams of conquest. The
true lover of peace, in spite of his evil traits, was Talleyrand.
From the very first day in the Ministry, he did everything in
his power to heal the wounds the French Revolution had
caused both at home and abroad.

Time and again, when differences arose between members
of the government, he poured oil on the troubled waters. It
was he, too, who tried to soothe the anger of the émigré
Royalists and persuade them to return to France and serve

their country. Understanding very clearly that it was French insistence on imposing her Republican ideas on her neighbors that had shattered European peace, he determined to put an end to this policy. He said that the only "useful and reasonable kind" of power, "the only kind befitting free and enlightened men is to be master at home and not to have the ridiculous pretension of ruling over others."

Peace was always foremost in Talleyrand's mind. During the early days of the Consulate his plans were all directed toward that goal. He worked tirelessly to end the state of war which existed between France and her neighbors, a war which had begun seven years before in 1792 when Louis XVI was still alive and on the throne and Danton was the spokesman of the Revolutionary government. But he was only one man, and against him were pitted many forces. So his first attempt at conciliation failed.

Determined to explore the possibility of an alliance between England and France, he sent a diplomatic note to England conveying the message that the First Consul desired to terminate the state of war which existed between the two countries and explore means of entering into friendly relations.

It was a reasonable and worthy gesture, but it brought a very arrogant and silly reply from the British government. France was advised that her first step toward peace should be to recall her legitimate and true monarch, Louis XVIII, the exiled brother of the beheaded Louis XVI and uncle of the lost Dauphin, Louis XVII.

This note piqued Talleyrand. He sent a biting reply. He reminded King George III that he had no right to demand legitimacy of France while the grandson of James II, the

rightful heir to the English throne, was living in exile in
Italy!

Talleyrand had failed in his attempt to terminate the state
of war existing with England and to win her friendship, but
he did not abandon hope. He would bide his time and someday . . . In the meantime he had other matters which needed
his attention. Napoleon had returned to Italy to regain the
kingdoms and other territories which had revolted against
French rule while he was in Egypt. He had defeated Austria
at Marengo and peace terms would soon have to be negotiated.

This was a pleasant prospect, one which Talleyrand welcomed almost as much as peace with England, for he felt
that Austria, acting as Europe's bulwark against invasion by
Russia, should be treated with the utmost care. She should
not be humiliated unnecessarily. France should not annex the
territories in northern Italy which she had won from Austria
and Sardinia. To do so would make Austria forever desirous
of revenge. Instead France should grant home rule to the
Italian states she had conquered, acting in the role of pro-
tector. To act otherwise, Talleyrand felt, would only an-
tagonize Austria and push her into the arms of Russia and
Prussia, that little kingdom to the far north which Talleyrand
very rightly envisioned as a future enemy of France.

Talleyrand was eager, indeed, to play a part in the coming
peace negotiations and the Treaty of Lunéville owes much to
his efforts, even though Napoleon, who always sought to
glorify himself and the members of his family, did not allow
Talleyrand to appear at any of the negotiations. While Austria acknowledged that Belgium, Luxembourg and the Piedmont were part of France, while she granted France all territories up to the Rhine and even some which lay beyond,

the Treaty of Lunéville placated Austria's feelings by declaring that Liguria and the Cisalpine Republic in northern Italy were independent states merely enjoying French protection. It went even further, recognizing the independence of Naples and only demanding that the king of that land maintain a French garrison at Taranto.

Through Talleyrand's astute negotiations at Lunéville, France had been elevated overnight to a first-class power; many of the lands she had conquered since 1792 had been formally acknowledged as hers, and her territory had thereby been greatly enlarged and extended to "natural boundaries," namely the Rhine and the Alps. Having such boundaries was, of course, a good thing for France and it had a stabilizing effect on the rest of Europe, for it was now believed that France would be satisfied to stay within her borders. Talleyrand felt that he had won an important point in his scheme for European peace.

There is no doubt that Talleyrand had won a great victory for France and Europe, but at Lunéville he also won something for himself—a very juicy plum. The Treaty of Lunéville granted France the right to help fix the indemnities to be granted the different German princes whose Rhenish territories had just been ceded to France. Several hundred small principalities would be reduced to about thirty sovereign states. Before such matters could be settled, many bribes and commissions would have to be paid and Talleyrand's wealth would be greatly increased. "This is the sort of work," a friend once wrote about Talleyrand, "which laid down the foundation of his immense fortune."

The Treaty of Lunéville had greatly increased France's territory and gained her an enviable position among the nations of Europe, but Napoleon was still not satisfied.

He disliked England. He considered her a "natural enemy" of France and had only consented with the greatest reluctance to Talleyrand's exploratory peace move of the previous year. Since it had failed so dismally he now determined to use force to bring England to terms.

To cross the Channel was less feasible now than it had been some years before when the Directory had asked Napoleon to undertake an invasion of the British Isles. The French fleet had been destroyed by Nelson on its return from Egypt and the British Navy now ruled the seas. And so Napoleon returned once more to his scheme of attacking England in the Orient. Only this time he would not do it alone, he would do it with the aid of Russia.

Against Talleyrand's advice, Napoleon had for the past year been wooing Czar Paul I and now his wily flatteries were about to bear fruit. The Czar cast aside his former allies, Austria and England, and entered into a treaty of friendship with France. Together Paul and Napoleon planned to drive the British from India! Did not Napoleon already have troops in Egypt?

Talleyrand was naturally deeply dismayed by Napoleon's plan. He spoke up boldly. He warned Napoleon against alliances with Russia and reminded him of the failure of his Egyptian campaign. He expressed the opinion that now that France had settled her boundaries and established peace with Austria, Napoleon would do best to concentrate on internal affairs. But Napoleon would not listen. He was overbearing. He was impulsive. He was obstinate. And a serious rift might have occurred between him and Talleyrand, had not Russia at that critical moment joined in an alliance with Prussia and the Scandinavian countries for the purpose of closing all the ports of northern Europe to British shipping.

Here was a scheme which met with Napoleon's approval.
In fact, he liked it so much that for the moment he forgot
about the Orient. What he now wanted was to have France
join the alliance, but this was met with disapproval from
Talleyrand, who insisted upon studying the matter. He said
that such a serious commitment required quiet contemplation. Napoleon was forced to wait, and while he was waiting,
events occurred which changed the entire situation and led
directly to a very advantageous peace for France with her
"natural enemy," England.

Just when relations between Napoleon and Paul I were at
their best, the Czar was assassinated—strangled by a group
of Russian army officers who distrusted Napoleon and the
influence he had on the Czar. His twenty-four-year-old son,
Alexander, who had encouraged the deed and was stanchly
pro-British, now became Czar of all the Russias. However,
this was not all. A few days after the assassination, Lord Nelson vanquished the Danish fleet and England once more became master of all northern European ports. Following close
upon this came the defeat by the British of Napoleon's ragged
and abandoned army in Egypt.

Talleyrand's caution and tactical delays had saved Napoleon and France untold problems. The French people were
now to be presented with an added bonus. The events
which had just occurred disposed both Napoleon and the
British to seek peace. Napoleon was all powerful on land
and England was all powerful at sea. They were powerless
to harm each other for the moment and so they might as well
be friends. After many months of negotiations the Treaty of
Amiens was finally signed by both countries on March 27,
1802.

Even though it was Napoleon's brother Joseph who signed

the Treaty of Amiens, it was, of course, Talleyrand who did all the work behind the scenes and it stands as a monument to his ability as a statesman. France won all sorts of concessions from England while forcing England to surrender most of the conquests she had made during the last ten years. Only Ceylon and Trinidad remained under the British flag.

England, at French insistence, returned to the Dutch the Cape of Good Hope and the colony of Demerara and the Island of Surinam in South America. France got back Martinique and Guadeloupe. And Malta was to be given back to the Order of St. John in Jerusalem.

France, on the other hand, did little more than agree to evacuate Taranto and a few other towns and small territories along the Mediterranean which she had occupied since Napoleon's second Italian campaign.

Because of Talleyrand's brilliance and ability France retained all the conquests she had made upon the Continent and which Austria had already recognized by the Treaty of Lunéville.

9.

Marriage

✦

Napoleon liked law and order, in spite of the violent methods
he had used to assume power. He, therefore, disapproved of
many of the methods which the Revolutionary governments
had used to achieve their ends. He also disapproved of some
of their reforms. The one which troubled him most was the
nationalization of the Church and he was determined from
the very first to make peace with Rome.

He was certain that Talleyrand, the ex-Bishop of Autun,
would guide him in this very delicate business. In fact, if
everything went as he hoped it would, the Pope might lift
the damnation of excommunication from Talleyrand and
eventually restore him to his position as bishop. In time he
might even be made a cardinal. Cardinals such as Richelieu
had served the kings of France as Ministers of State. Why
then, should not his Minister of Foreign Affairs be a cardinal? These were the thoughts that possessed Napoleon, for
he was driven with ambition and envisioned himself as becoming the sole ruler of France. Now that he was First Consul
he was planning to get rid of the two other Consuls and rule
alone!

Napoleon believed that Talleyrand would be glad to help him in his negotiations with Rome, but he was wrong. Talleyrand had several reasons for wanting to let matters remain as they were. And so from the beginning the negotiations were fraught with problems.

In the first place, Talleyrand felt, "Those whom the Revolution pardons must pardon the Revolution." By that he meant that Rome must not expect France to come as a penitent willing to atone for her sins. Instead Rome and France must meet as equals and for the sole purpose of reaching an "understanding" or "settlement."

In the second place, Talleyrand was determined that if the Church were to be re-established in France, he, Talleyrand, ex-Bishop of Autun, must be completely forgiven by Rome for all his past conduct. He must be relieved of all guilt for having broken his vows and for having nationalized Church property and helped to establish the "Constitutional Church."

Added to these two reasons was a third, which was not discussed openly but over which Napoleon and Talleyrand snarled at each other like two dogs with one bone. Talleyrand was in love with a woman whom Napoleon detested and he was planning to marry her! Her name was Catherine Grand and she had come into Talleyrand's life some years before while he was Minister of Foreign Affairs for the Directory. In order to marry her, Talleyrand wanted Rome to free him from his vows as priest and bishop and return him to the status of a simple citizen.

Catherine was an extraordinarily beautiful woman, and although she was only thirty-five years old when Talleyrand first met her, she had already led a very full and adventurous life. She was French but had been born in India where her parents made their home. At the age of fifteen she had married an Englishman named Grand, who was a high-ranking official of the East India Company in Calcutta. Grand had a salary equivalent to $50,000 a year in our modern money, and his social position was second only to that of the British governor-general. Catherine Grand enjoyed the greatest luxuries which India could provide.

However, Catherine's marriage to Mr. Grand did not last very long. Within five years, the ravishing Madame Grand left her husband and went to live in France. Then during the Revolution she fled to England. However, she was back in Paris when Talleyrand returned from America and so it happened that their paths chanced to cross.

One evening, after he had eaten his supper and played a game of whist with three members of his staff, Talleyrand was about to retire when a servant announced that a lady, bearing a letter of introduction, was waiting for him in the reception hall of the Ministry.

Talleyrand was annoyed, for the hour was late and he was weary. He was in a very bad humor when he made his way to the far end of the mansion and into the reception hall of the Ministry.

There before the open fire, wrapped in a great cloak and curled up in one of the deep chairs, was a young woman, fast asleep. As he came forward to look more closely, she suddenly awakened and jumped to her feet. She was tall and supple, her skin was pale and radiant, her eyes were large and blue, her slightly turned-up nose gave her an air of proud distinction. A great shock of blonde hair framed her face.

Her story was long and filled with troubles. All her attempts to recover her property, which had been confiscated by the Revolution when she fled to England, had failed. She was having difficulty with her passport and now she was accused of espionage and was being followed by the police. She feared she would be arrested and imprisoned.

Her eyes filled with tears as she insisted upon her innocence and appealed to Talleyrand for advice and protection. He alone, she felt, had the power to help her.

Talleyrand was greatly moved by her beauty and her story and immediately called on Barras, one of the Five Directors, to have the charges against Catherine Grand dropped. He was forty-three, she was thirty-five, and he was now madly in love with her. They spent many hours alone, but he also invited her to all his parties large and small, even though his friends ridiculed her silly remarks, her lack of education and her bad grammar. Catherine was beautiful beyond compare, but she was not very bright.

Napoleon was one of the few who did not object to Catherine's stupidity. He disliked her for a different reason. He considered her an adventuress, and since he was trying to lift French morals from the low state into which they had fallen under the Bourbons and during the Revolution, he did not feel that she was a fit companion for his Minister of Foreign Affairs. She was less acceptable to him as Talleyrand's wife.

And so Napoleon and Talleyrand feuded with each other and the negotiations with Rome suffered. In spite of this, certain basic issues were finally settled. It was agreed between Rome and France that religious freedom for all, as guaranteed by the Revolution, would be preserved but that the Catholic Church would be re-established in France as the Church "of the majority." It was further agreed that bishops were to be nominated by the government, but the Pope was to confer the office. Parish priests were to be chosen by the bishops with the approval of the government. Confiscated Church property which had been sold to private persons was not to be re-

turned to the Church, but as a compensation the State was to
support the clergy.

In other words, all matters were satisfactorily settled except those relating personally to Talleyrand.

Napoleon wanted Talleyrand to put aside his beloved
Catherine, and ask forgiveness of Rome. Talleyrand wanted
only to be released of all guilt and freed from his vows so that
he could marry. With his genius for wording documents,
Talleyrand attempted repeatedly to get the Vatican to sign an
agreement allowing certain members of the clergy to marry.
Rome remained unmoved. And the agreement or "Concor-
dat" between the Vatican and France was finally signed without his having gained his point.

Talleyrand had lost, but he would not give up. He wrote
directly to the Pope admitting that he had committed certain
very serious "errors" and asked that the Pope release him
from all his vows and allow him to return to the status of lay-
man with the privilege of partaking in communion. He also
prevailed upon Napoleon to plead with the Pope in his behalf. Napoleon's appeal stated among other things that Talleyrand had worked tirelessly for two years to re-establish the
legitimate Catholic Church in France and that he therefore
deserved the "greatest condescension."

The Pope finally acquiesced, but only to a degree. He
signed a "brief of reconciliation" in which he absolved Talleyrand, the sinner, of "all the censures which bind him."

Talleyrand was not satisfied and the battle continued. To
settle the matter the Pope finally wrote saying that he could
not release Talleyrand of his sacred vows because in eighteen
centuries, "there does not exist one single example of dispen-
sation being granted to a consecrated bishop in order that he
may marry."

The matter seemed closed, but not to Talleyrand. He persisted, and was finally granted certain concessions. He was returned to communion and, henceforth, allowed to wear civilian dress and accept public duties, two things which he had been indulging in since the day he took his vows as priest! But he still could not marry.

Tired of the whole argument, Napoleon now took the matter into his own hands. He tampered a bit with the truth and printed an announcement in the French press saying that on June 29, 1802, by special permission of the Pope, "Charles Maurice de Talleyrand, Minister of Foreign Affairs, was restored in full to lay and secular life."

Talleyrand knew that the Pope had done no such thing. However, he pretended to believe that such a release had truly been granted him, a pretension in which he was to persist until the last day of his life! On September 19, at the city hall in Paris he married "Catherine-Noel Worlée, 39 . . . the divorced wife of George Francis Grand." Among those who signed the marriage contract were Josephine and Napoleon Bonaparte, First Consul of France.

Even though Napoleon had an intense dislike of Catherine, he had finally made her marriage to Talleyrand possible. However, he now decreed that she was forbidden ever to enter the Tuileries, where he and Josephine lived, except on state occasions and in her official capacity as the wife of his Minister of Foreign Affairs, Charles Maurice de Talleyrand.

10.

A Crime—A Blunder

⚜

The Treaty of Amiens, ending the war with England, was hailed as a triumph of statesmanship in all parts of France. To show the gratitude of the people of France for this success, the Senate re-elected Napoleon as First Consul for a second ten-year term to begin when his present ten-year term drew to an end.

Napoleon was flattered by this honor, but he was also deeply disappointed. He had hoped that the Senate would proclaim him sole ruler of France, so he entered into collusion with certain members of the government to hold a referendum on the question, "Is Napoleon Bonaparte to be made Consul for life?" The people responded with an overwhelming vote of three and a half million "for" and only eight and a half thousand "against" the proposition.

Having gained the victory Napoleon immediately changed the Constitution. All vestiges of democratic processes were eliminated and succession was made hereditary. In short, Napoleon now had the powers of an absolute monarch!

From the very first, Napoleon had dreamed of being sole ruler of France. Talleyrand had favored this idea. He had remained true to his belief that a constitutional monarchy like England's was the best form of government; and fearing that if the Bourbons were restored he would have to leave the country because of the part he had played in the Revolution, he had pinned his hopes on Napoleon.

Working toward this end, Talleyrand had helped him by manipulating political affairs behind the scenes. He had contributed immeasurably to the presentation of the referendum. He also helped enormously by introducing the coarsely bred young Corsican and his large family of brothers and sisters to the highest French society.

He gave elegant parties for Napoleon at the Ministry and at his home. Implementing his belief that "Those who have been forgiven by the Revolution, must forgive the Revolution," he always made certain that there were Royalist émigrés present, gentlemen and ladies who had once served at Versailles and who had now returned from exile. Indeed, it was due greatly to Talleyrand's efforts that Napoleon became more and more regal each day and that the Tuileries took on once more the elegance of a royal court.

Napoleon and Talleyrand worked so closely and intently together on re-establishing the throne in France that their ambition soon broke all restraints. By the end of 1803 they were preparing the way for Napoleon's eventual crowning as Emperor! And it was in the pursuit of this glorification that they became involved in a dark and ugly deed. Fouché, Napoleon's sinister Minister of Police, said that their deed was "worse than a crime—a blunder."

Talleyrand felt that to elevate Napoleon to Emperor it was absolutely necessary to have the support not only of the Royalists but also of the most ardent of the former Revolutionists. To win their confidence, Napoleon would have to give them convincing proof that he was in full sympathy with all they had done, including executing Louis XVI. What greater proof could they receive than to have Napoleon also execute a Bourbon? By doing this Napoleon would place himself "on their level" and make himself "one of them." And so with this foremost in his thoughts, Talleyrand began to prepare a heinous plot against the life of an innocent man, the Duke d'Enghien.

Toward the end of January, 1804, a conspiracy against Napoleon's life was uncovered in Paris. Some of those involved had been members of the former Revolutionary government; others were Royalists. Napoleon was unnerved by the whole affair. However, he was satisfied with the arrest of the conspirators and was more than willing to forget the whole business. He would have done just that had not Talleyrand come to him with a long and evil story concerning the young Duke d'Enghien, a cousin of the beheaded Louis XVI and a member of the Condé branch of the Bourbons, who was visiting in Baden just across the Rhine.

Talleyrand said that it had been discovered that the young Count was involved with the assassination plot and that he was at that very moment still engaged in talks with some of the conspirators who had not been apprehended. He recommended most urgently that an example be made of the Count. He advised Napoleon to have him brought into France, tried and executed.

At first Napoleon doubted the whole story and very rightly so, for the young Duke was completely innocent. He was in Baden because he was in love with a young princess of Baden and not because of a plot against Napoleon's life. However, Talleyrand was not to be put off. He persisted until Napoleon truly believed that the young man was involved, but Napoleon refused to do anything about it. He said that since Baden was beyond the French border, he could not interfere.

Josephine, who learned of the conversations between Talleyrand and Napoleon, pleaded with her husband not to kill the innocent Count. She threw herself at Napoleon's feet, weeping and cajoling, but Talleyrand, who saw Napoleon every day, managed to counteract her influence. By his very persistence, he was slowly breaking down Napoleon's resistance.

And so the dreadful deed was done. Napoleon ordered a small raiding party to violate the neutrality of Baden, kidnap the Duke and bring him into France. He was taken to the Castle of Vincennes just outside of Paris. His grave had already been dug, so his trial was very brief and his conviction certain. He was executed in the dry moat of the ancient castle at half-past two the following morning.

Talleyrand, who was playing whist at a friend's home that night, looked at his watch at that very moment and said, "The last Condé has ceased to exist."

The following day when the news of the execution appeared in the press, everyone referred to the murder as a most sinister deed. Talleyrand, however, rubbed it off, saying, "Oh, well, business is business." When Czar Alexander demanded an explanation from the French government, Talleyrand, as French Minister of Foreign Affairs, replied that as far as he knew nobody had ever been punished for the murder of the Czar Paul, his late father. This was a very bold remark; Talleyrand wanted to remind Emperor Alexander that no one had forgotten that he was himself involved in the strangling of his father.

It was soon obvious that a serious blunder had been made, and Napoleon as head of the government, of course, had to accept full responsibility. Privately he said, "It was Talley-rand who made me decide to arrest the Duke d'Enghien." Later a friend heard him say, "I find it amusing that Talley-rand plays his tricks at my expense. Did I know the Duke d'Enghien? Was it I who wanted him killed?"

Everyone was deeply shocked by what had happened. Josephine said, "That cripple makes me tremble." But Barras, who knew the reason why Talleyrand had gone to such lengths, put it very simply. He said, "Talleyrand wanted to put a river of blood between Napoleon and the Bourbons."

He was correct. Less than nine months later, on December 2, 1804, Napoleon Bonaparte was crowned Emperor of France at a magnificent coronation ceremony at Notre Dame.

11.

Of Châteaux, Vast Fortunes and Princely Titles

✦

"He would sell his soul," said a contemporary speaking of Talleyrand. By that he meant that Talleyrand demanded a price for every duty he performed.

During the few months that he served as Minister of Foreign Affairs to the Directory, Talleyrand amassed more than ten million livres, or the equivalent of two million dollars. One trade treaty which he negotiated at that time brought him two and one half million livres! Very cynically, he once remarked, "I have been paid only for what I should have done without being paid."

During the five years of the Consulate, 1799–1804, he is said to have amassed forty million livres. When the Treaty of Lunéville was being drawn up, he received over fifteen million livres from Austria alone.

It was a time of upheaval in Europe. Boundaries were not firmly established. A fresh war might deprive a state of thousands of square miles and millions of souls. Because of the position France had gained at Lunéville and Amiens, the

First Consul of France was often the sole arbitrator of who should gain and who should lose. He left these details to his Minister of Foreign Affairs, and Talleyrand was careful to collect what he called "tidbits" from everyone concerned.

All Europe was eager to gain his good will. There was not a diplomat who dared approach France without gold in his hand, because Talleyrand had very cleverly created the impression that Napoleon would do nothing without him. "Despite his feeble appearance," wrote one such statesman, "he leads both his master and Europe."

Diplomatic maneuvers provided Talleyrand with enormous wealth, but that was not all. He invested in the stock market. His position gave him an advantage. He knew in advance if a peace treaty would be signed or if war would be declared. He also had advance knowledge on all trade treaties and other developments which affect a nation's economy.

However, while it is true that Talleyrand loved wealth and accumulated a great fortune during these opening years of his career as Minister of Foreign Affairs, he did not hoard all his money. He spent a great deal—for comforts, for pleasures and for the gracious life.

While serving the Directory he gave a great party to introduce the young Bonaparte, hero of the Italian campaign, to Paris society. It was held in the great palace of the Foreign Ministry on the Rue de Bac; it was a dazzling affair. The next day a lady of his acquaintance said to him, "That must have cost you dear."

"Oh, it was nothing at all. Nothing," he replied.

It was later learned that this party had cost Talleyrand half a million livres! But as he said, it was really nothing, for this party was only one of many such receptions he gave on the Rue de Bac.

On the evenings of Talleyrand's great parties, the Rue de
Bac would be so crowded that the elegant coaches and carriages were forced to line up for several blocks. They moved
very slowly toward the entrance where the guests alit, aided
by footmen and doormen dressed in the livery of the Talley-
rand-Périgords'.

Inside a small regiment of lackeys in the same livery lined
the way to the grand marble stairway through the great hall,
flooded with the light of hundreds of candles and decorated
with great banks of flowers.

Bejeweled ladies in magnificent gowns, accompanied by
gentlemen in uniforms decorated with shining orders,
mounted the great stairway with measured and stately dignity. Talleyrand waited at the top to receive them, and although he was slight of build and crippled and had to use a
cane, he presented a proud figure, his pale face providing a
startling contrast to the brilliant vermilion of his official min-
isterial uniform.

When Napoleon came into power there were more and
more foreign officials to be entertained. Napoleon recognized
this; he even encouraged it. He also knew that Talleyrand
could not possibly pay for all these evenings out of his salary,
and so he closed his eyes to Talleyrand's grasping ways. Only
occasionally did Napoleon chide Talleyrand.

He once asked him where he got his great wealth. "I
bought stocks before the *coup d'état* and sold them after you
stabilized the government," Talleyrand answered. And Napoleon, thoroughly flattered, probed no further.

Under the Consulate, Talleyrand had bought a mansion in
Paris and two splendid villas in the suburbs. To run such es-
tablishments he had had to support a whole regiment of

lackeys in livery and a small army of apron men and women: grooms, porters, gardeners, laborers and maids and cooks.

Talleyrand eventually sold his two villas and bought a fine estate in Neuilly on the outskirts of Paris. It was there in the parklike grounds that he gave a famous party for the Prince of Parma and the Infanta of Spain.

The setting had been prepared with the greatest elaboration. The grounds were illuminated with hundreds of shielded candles and lamps whose light lent a touch of magic. There were painted backdrops, like those used on the stage, of famous Florentine buildings including the Pitti Palace. The musicians played old Italian music on rare instruments. There were dancers in native costumes, street singers and troubadours. Three different suppers were brought into the gardens and served between midnight and the early morning hours. Several orchestras played and the dancing continued until sunrise.

This was a party that cost more than half a million! But Talleyrand did not care. He always spent lavishly.

He rarely sat down to dinner with less than forty or fifty invited guests. There were sometimes a hundred or more. One of the guests, an English lady, described one of his dinners: "I never saw anything so magnificent—the apartments beautiful, all perfumed with frankincense. And as soon as seventy-eight people, of which the company consisted, sat down, an immense mirror at the end of the room slid away by degrees and soft and beautiful music began to play in the midst of the jingle of glasses and dishes."

Yes, Napoleon knew that Talleyrand made "a bargain sale" of the affairs of state to pay for his opulent living, but he never complained. He felt that the money Talleyrand gained for himself was unimportant compared to the good he did for

France. Napoleon was ever conscious of the fact that during the first two years that Talleyrand served him as Minister of Foreign Affairs, France had been raised from humiliation to a position of the highest importance among the nations of Europe. Napoleon was well aware too that it was the treaties which Talleyrand had negotiated behind the scenes at Lunéville and Amiens, following his victories in the field, that had ended discord in Europe and brought the glow of glory once more to France.

It must also be stated here that while there are many records of Talleyrand's dishonorable dealings there is not one in which he profited at the cost of France. One thing remained sacred to Talleyrand to his dying day—France.

Napoleon not only knew where Talleyrand got the fabulous sums which he spent, but from time to time he actually gave Talleyrand large sums from the Treasury. He did this for two reasons: he wanted a Minister who could present an elegant front to foreign powers; he needed Talleyrand's help in furthering his own dreams of royalty, for Napoleon was building up a new nobility to replace the heads that had fallen during the Revolution. Besides the Tuileries, he now used the royal palace of Fontainebleau; and he had created a court with a Grand Chamberlain and all the other regal functionaries and surrounded Josephine with gracious ladies-in-waiting.

He had made his brothers kings and his sisters queens. His generals became princes and dukes and their wives, regardless of their lowly birth, became princesses and duchesses. The Duchess of Leipzig had once been a washerwoman and had later fought beside her husband during the Revolution and on the battlefields that brought victory to Napoleon. She was proud of being a duchess and considered the honor bestowed upon her as a just one.

It was also during these early years when Napoleon needed Talleyrand so desperately that he one day said to him, "I would like to see you buy a fine property, a place where you can give brilliant receptions for the diplomatic corps and for distinguished foreign visitors, so that everyone will want to visit you there. An invitation to such a place, as I have in mind, would be a sort of reward for the ambassadors and sovereigns who have my approval."

A friend who was present suggested that Talleyrand buy the Château of Valençay situated about 140 miles due south from Paris. This historic castle and its estate, which covered a full eighty square miles of old forests and fields, were for sale because since the Revolution they had become a burden to the owners. The price was 1,600,000 livres.

Talleyrand protested, saying that he could not possibly afford such an estate, but Napoleon was not to be put off. He offered to help Talleyrand pay for the fine château. In the end Napoleon paid for most of it!

Napoleon was ever generous, not only with money but with rewards and titles. And it was at this period that he bestowed the highest order of the Legion of Honor upon Talleyrand and made him Grand Chamberlain of his court. This and more. Since Talleyrand had been deprived of his rightful title of Prince because of the injury which had left him lame, Napoleon decided to give Talleyrand what his parents had denied him. He made him Prince of Benevento, a small Italian principality in the kingdom of Naples.

Talleyrand received his new title graciously. He was genuinely happy that Napoleon had recognized his work and valued his services so much. Madame Talleyrand was de-

lighted to be a princess. Still he felt a little awkward with an
Italian title. After all, he had been born a French prince—he
considered this a much higher mark of distinction. More
than once, during diplomatic discussions, when he was addressed as "Your Highness," he politely expressed the wish
to be called simply, "Monsieur de Talleyrand." And once,
commenting on his Italian title, he said, "I am less, and perhaps I am even more."

12.

Prelude to Treason

❧

Talleyrand was a master of intrigue and diplomacy. He could outmaneuver the most capable men in France and Europe. He had tremendous powers of persuasion. However, there was one man with whom he sometimes found it impossible to deal and that man was Napoleon.

Within a year of signing the Treaties of Lunéville and Amiens, and against Talleyrand's sage advice, Napoleon plunged France once more into war.

While England and Austria and all the other kingdoms of Europe watched in bewilderment, Napoleon quietly went about his evil work. He effected changes in the Dutch Constitution which placed power in the hands of pro-French elements in Holland and enabled him to keep French troops in the most important Dutch fortresses. Through secret manipulations he then had himself elected president of the Cisalpine Republic. After that he issued a decree making Piedmont a military district wholly dependent on France. He then reduced the Genoese Republic to a puppet state and transformed Tuscany into the kingdom of Etruria placing the

Duke of Parma at its head. He interfered in Swiss internal troubles, sending French troops in to occupy that land.

Talleyrand tried desperately to get Napoleon to withdraw his troops from Holland and Switzerland as England demanded. Napoleon refused to listen. In vain Talleyrand tried to impress upon him the wisdom of a strong alliance between England and France. In vain did he point out the futility of war. "M. de Talleyrand is in despair," wrote an associate, "and if he still could either prevent the crash or stop the course of events . . . he would consider this feat one of the most glorious of his Ministry."

Talleyrand's efforts did not succeed because Napoleon, without consulting him, had decided to return to his plan of driving England out of India. To accomplish this he hurriedly engaged in a vast program of building up the French Army and constructing a Navy. He raised money by extracting huge sums through coercion from such states as Hanover, Naples, Portugal and Spain, which had a mutual assistance pact with France. By selling the Territory of Louisiana, including New Orleans, to the United States he added 60,000,-000 francs more to his war chest.

When the French and Indian Wars ended in America in 1763, France had lost all her possessions east of the Mississippi with the exception of New Orleans. A few years later she lost this city and all her land west of the Mississppi, the Louisiana Territory, to Spain. When Napoleon came into power, he demanded that Spain return New Orleans and Louisiana to France, and Spain, helpless to resist, complied.

Napoleon planned to send a military force across the Atlantic to occupy this territory. The young United States was greatly disturbed. Thomas Jefferson, who was then President, was particularly upset at the thought of having such an aggressive power as France as a neighbor. He feared that with New Orleans in French hands, that great port and the Mississippi River might be closed to American commerce; many new American states bordered the eastern shore of the Mississippi. He feared that it might lead to war, and so he sent Monroe to France to join Livingston, our Ambassador in Paris, with instructions to buy New Orleans for a sum not to exceed ten million dollars.

Jefferson's worries were unnecessary because he did not know about Napoleon's plans and his great need of money. Before Monroe reached France, Talleyrand had visited Livingston and offered him New Orleans and the entire Territory of Louisiana for 100,000,000 francs or $25,000,000.

Monroe arrived the very next day. This sum was more than Jefferson had authorized for New Orleans alone, but the territory was much greater. Monroe and Livingston did not know what to do. It would have taken sixty days to send a letter to President Jefferson and receive a reply. They decided to act on their own, and after two weeks of bargaining with Talleyrand a price was decided upon—60,000,000 francs or about $15,000,000.

When Monroe and Livingston asked Talleyrand about the extent of the Louisiana Territory he was unable to give them a reply. "There is no map," he said, "but gentlemen you have made a bargain, make the best of it."

Talleyrand did not know that with one stroke of the pen the territory of the United States had just been doubled. Out of the Louisiana Territory were carved thirteen states and a part of Texas—828,000 square miles for less than four cents an acre.

And so within a year after Napoleon had crowned himself Emperor, France was once more at war with England. However, if it was Napoleon's wish to fight England alone, he was to be disappointed. Russia and Austria, fearing that they might be next, joined England.

As might have been expected, England fared very well in her war against France because she fought her at sea. She won quick victories against French squadrons and colonies, especially in the West Indies. Then in 1805, the British fleet under Nelson completely vanquished the French fleet at the battle of Trafalgar off the southern coast of Spain.

It was on land that Napoleon distinguished himself, and Austria bore the brunt of his attacks. His spectacular victories at Ulm and Austerlitz brought Austria to her knees.

Talleyrand, who valued Austria almost as highly as England as an ally of France, decided to try once more before it was too late to bring Napoleon to reason. He pointed out that Europe consisted of four great powers: France, England, Austria and Russia. Prussia and the German states were not yet consolidated and so he did not count them. Of these four powers he considered France as the greatest in both men and money. But while she was stronger than any other, he pointed out to Napoleon that she was not powerful enough to withstand an attack if England, Russia and Austria should ever join their armies. Besides, Austria was in the best position to thwart Russian expansion into western Europe and she alone could stop Russian and English designs in the East.

Therefore, Talleyrand reasoned, it was important to break Austria's ties to Russia and England, and he proposed that Napoleon win her over by granting her a generous peace. Also Austria should be encouraged to expand her dominion —not in western Europe, of course, but at the expense of

Turkey, in the Balkans. Her interests would then lie in eastern Europe. She would in no way threaten France but would instead worry Russia. Victory on the battlefield would thus be followed by victory at the peace table. Austria would become a friend of France and an enemy of France's enemy, Russia.

Talleyrand's plan was a brilliant piece of statesmanship. However, Napoleon would not listen to the logical reasoning of his shrewd Minister. He rejected it without reservations. Knowing that he risked Napoleon's disfavor, Talleyrand tried once again. At the very last minute, December 5, 1805, he wrote Napoleon a letter: "Your Majesty may now destroy the Austrian monarchy or raise it up. Once destroyed, it will not be re-established. Preserve it. Stretch out a generous hand. . . . France is great enough. If Austria is too much weakened in the east she will not have the means to keep control. . . . The Russians will become all powerful in Europe. I beg Your Majesty to reconsider the plan which I had the honor to address to him. . . ."

It was an urgent plea, but Napoleon tossed it aside. And so, since Ministers often carry out policies in which they do not personally agree, Talleyrand was forced to preside at the Peace of Pressburg and impose upon Austria conditions which he deplored, conditions which reduced the Austrian empire to a shadow of its former glory and planted the political ground with seeds of still another war.

Austria was forced to recognize all the recent changes in Italy and surrender Venetia, Istria and Dalmatia. She was also forced to cede certain large territories to South German states which had helped Napoleon in the war, and the Electors of Bavaria and Württemberg were recognized as kings. This meant that the Emperor Francis lost three million sub-

jects and one-sixth of all his revenues. He was also required to
pay an indemnity of forty million francs. But even this severe
treaty did not fully satisfy Napoleon. He accused Talleyrand
of being too lenient with Austria.

Drunk with success Napoleon now punished Prussia because she had been preparing to come to Austria's aid. At
sword's point, he forced Prussia to exclude all British shipping from the northwest coast of Germany, thus ruining
Prussian economy. He then gave Anspach and Bayreuth to
Bavaria. To further strengthen his ties of friendship with the
South German states he arranged marriages between his step-
son, Eugene, Josephine's son by her first marriage, and the
daughter of the King of Bavaria; his brother Jerome Bonaparte and the daughter of the King of Württemberg; and
Josephine's niece, Stephanie, and the son of the Grand Duke
of Baden.

But there was more to come. A few months later he
grouped all the princes of southern and central Germany into
the Confederation of the Rhine and placed them under his
"protection." He made Josephine's son Eugene ruler of
Milan, his brother Joseph King of the Two Sicilies, his
brother-in-law Murat ruler of the Duchy of Berg, and his
brother Louis King of Holland! "I am making a family of
kings," he said.

Napoleon now controlled all the lands from the Elbe to
the Pyrenees and had Italy completely under his control. But
while he was in the most optimistic mood, Talleyrand was in
the deepest gloom. He knew it meant another war. And he
began to wonder at what manner of man this was whom he
had helped bring to power.

The war Talleyrand knew would result from the Peace of
Pressburg was not long in coming. Prussia, which had been so

badly treated, now joined with Russia, Austria and England, and in 1806 Europe once more resounded with the roar of cannon and the cries of the dying.

Talleyrand was more distressed than ever, but Napoleon, who had a passion for conquest, plunged into bloody battle with the greatest satisfaction. He fought Prussia first, completing a dramatic and victorious campaign against her in less than forty days. He then engaged the Russians. He planned that when they begged for mercy he would throw all his weight against England.

Napoleon insisted on having his chief Ministers close at hand. And so their carriages rode on in the wake of death from battlefield to battlefield. In one place Talleyrand encountered "four thousand wounded." At another time he recorded, "there are many deaths every day." It was all too strenuous for a man who loved leisure, luxury and quiet contemplation. Besides, his crippled foot was giving him a great deal of pain. Still, pen in hand, he was compelled to follow along as Napoleon added one victory to another: Jena, Berlin, Eylau, Friedland.

On and on his carriage swayed and rattled over the terrible roads of East Germany and Poland. Again and again he argued with the Emperor that conquered lands lead only to unrest; that people crushed and humiliated by defeat and forced to pay heavy indemnities were certain to revolt; that the French Army was not big enough to police every square mile of Europe. The Emperor neither listened nor heard, and so once again at Tilsit as at Pressburg, Napoleon dictated a "peace" which could only lead to more war, a "peace" which partitioned Poland and imposed a staggering indemnity upon Prussia and which struck at England by demanding that the Scandinavian countries close all their ports to British trade.

As though this were not enough, Napoleon then entered into an agreement which Talleyrand advised strongly against. With promises of political and territorial gains, he wooed Russia away from England and Austria, and then joined her in an alliance against her former friends, England, Austria and Prussia.

"I do not know where common sense has taken refuge," Talleyrand wrote to a friend.

The Peace of Pressburg had caused a rift between Napoleon and Talleyrand. This rift had been widened by the peace at Tilsit, and Talleyrand realized that he could not continue as Minister of Foreign Affairs when all his advice was being brushed aside and he was constantly being forced to draw up documents and sign agreements which were contrary to everything in which he believed.

He knew this, yet he hated to sever his connections because he truly liked the Emperor. "I was fond of Napoleon," he later wrote. "I was attached to his person notwithstanding his faults. When he first appeared on the scene of the world, I felt attracted towards him by the irresistible spell inherent to great genius. I was sincerely grateful to him for the favors he had bestowed on me. . . . I shared in his glory, which reflected on all those who assisted in his . . . work."

Yes, Talleyrand knew that he would have to leave, yet he hesitated, hoping that Napoleon might give up conquest and concentrate on building France into a great and prosperous nation. After the victory over the Russians at Friedland, he sent Napoleon a note, saying, "I like to think of this victory as the last one which Your Majesty will be forced to win. For that reason it is dear to me; for, splendid as it is, I must declare that it would lose more in my sight than I can say if Your Majesty had to march on to new battles . . ."

In fact, it was not until the day that Napoleon confided in him that with Prussia, Russia and Austria at his feet, he was now determined to destroy the Bourbon dynasty in Spain, that Talleyrand knew this was the end of their relationship. "It was then," he has recorded, "that I determined that I would cease to be his Minister as soon as we returned to France."

The revelation of Napoleon's secret plans had determined Talleyrand's immediate future. It had done more than that. It had sealed the fate of Europe, because in that instant Talleyrand also realized that if Europe was to know peace, Napoleon must be destroyed. An end must be called to this insanity. He decided that he, Charles Maurice de Talleyrand-Périgord, would bring about Napoleon's downfall!

He laid his plans carefully. Returning to Paris in the opening months of 1808, he resigned as Minister of Foreign Affairs, but not before he had himself promoted to the office of Vice-Grand Elector, the third highest post in the government, a post which guaranteed him an active role in European politics.

Not suspecting Talleyrand's purpose, Napoleon had eagerly accepted his resignation. He too was anxious for a change. He looked forward to having a Minister of Foreign Affairs whose views were more in harmony with his own, but wishing to retain the prestige of Talleyrand's name in the government, he gladly elevated him to Vice-Grand Elector with the title of Most Serene Highness and a salary of 500,000 livres a year.

The stage was now set. The conflict was about to begin. A

slight, pale aristocrat in delicate health and with a crippled foot would encounter the powerful and still youthful Emperor Napoleon, crusher of armies and destroyer of nations. It seemed an uneven match and the struggle would be long and fierce, but it would change the course of history.

13.

The Spanish Affair

❧

Napoleon was at the height of his power when Talleyrand decided to bring about his destruction. Most of Europe was under his rule. His empire rivaled the empires of Alexander the Great and Charlemagne. Yet Talleyrand was not dismayed. Slowly and patiently and in a most devious manner did he begin the herculean task of breaking up the empire and bringing Napoleon to ruin.

He proceeded with the utmost caution. He secretly let it be known in certain diplomatic circles, especially in Vienna, that he would no longer support his Emperor's irresponsible actions. He let it be known that he had always disapproved of the terms of Pressburg and Tilsit. In short, he let Napoleon's enemies know that they had "a friend" in Paris. While he always denied it, historical records seem to indicate that he began his dark treachery with the Spanish Affair. While he took no active part in the Spanish Affair, these records indicate that he encouraged Napoleon to launch an attack against Spain, believing that once the Emperor was embroiled he could be counted upon to do himself immeasurable harm.

The members of the Spanish royal house were Bourbons.

Their ancestors had been placed upon the Spanish throne by
Louis XIV. Talleyrand is reported to have repeatedly main-
tained that Napoleon should do away with them and take
over all their possessions. He is quoted as saying over and
over again, "Since the days of Louis XIV, the crown of Spain
has belonged to the family which reigned in France. . . . It is
one of the best parts of the heritage of Louis XIV and the
Emperor ought to gather up this entire heritage. He ought
not to give up one single part of it.'

Napoleon, of course, liked to hear Talleyrand speak in this
manner. Besides he felt that he had a good reason for invading
Spain; Spain, his ally, had betrayed him. A letter was found
among the papers left behind by the fleeing King of Prussia
in which Spain offered Prussia help against France. It promised that with the first Prussian victory, Spain would attack
France from the rear!

Everything and everyone seemed to lend support to Napoleon's wishes—even the Spanish royal family which was floun-
dering about in a state of dismal decay. The King, who had
always been slightly feeble-minded, was now senile. The
Queen, who was healthy but ignorant, had made one of her
intimate friends, Godoy, Prime Minister, and this evil man
was blocking every effort by Ferdinand, the twenty-four-year-
old Crown Prince, to get his father to abdicate in his favor.

The situation seemed right for Napoleon. Under the pretext of punishing Portugal for having an alliance with Britain
and letting her use Portuguese ports, Napoleon gained permission from Spain to send an army across her territory.
Portugal was to be partitioned and Spain was to receive half
of her territory as a reward. Part of this army went to Portugal as agreed upon, but another section, 40,000 men, swept
through northern and western Spain, until it reached Madrid!

The Spanish people, completely deluded, thought that Napoleon had sent his troops to help free them from Godoy, whom they hated. They revolted, forced Godoy out and made the old King abdicate in favor of Ferdinand.

The old King protested and Napoleon, posing as a "friend," offered to act as arbiter. All the Spanish royal family had to do was to meet with him on French soil just over the Spanish border!

Surprising as it may seem, Napoleon's offer was accepted, and the Spanish royal family crossed the Pyrenees to Bayonne. That was the last they saw of Spain for many, many years, because Napoleon frightened Ferdinand into returning the crown to his senile father, by threatening him with a trial for high treason, and then made the old King abdicate in his, Napoleon's, favor.

Once this had been accomplished, the King and Queen of Spain were "allowed" to go to Italy, where they eventually ended their days. However, a better fate befell Ferdinand, his younger brother and an uncle who had also come to Bayonne. They were "imprisoned" in Talleyrand's magnificent château at Valençay.

While Napoleon had, in a sense, welcomed Talleyrand's resignation from the Ministry, he had also looked upon it as a rejection, an insult. He was piqued and he wanted to insult him in turn. He would make the haughty and elegant Talleyrand act as a jailor!

He wrote a long letter of instructions: "I wish these princes to be received with no outward ceremony, but decently, and that you do everything possible to entertain them. See that the rooms are ready, prepare the beds and table linen."

Talleyrand was not only surprised but also shocked at Napoleon's letter. However, he never let the Emperor know that he considered his act rude and insulting. Being a supreme diplomat he wrote very politely, "I will respond with my best endeavors to the confidence with which your Majesty honors me. Mme. de Talleyrand left last night to give the preliminary orders. The Château is amply furnished with cooks, china and linen of all kinds."

Having disposed of the Spanish royal family, Napoleon placed his eldest brother Joseph upon the throne of Spain. But it was not so easy to dispose of the Spanish people, and King Joseph had to be supported by French troops. Even then the Spaniards managed to organize a mass revolt. They were proud of their past and loved their royal family and their country. They hated the French conquerors and fought with such passion that Napoleon himself was finally forced to lead an army into Spain to try to restore order.

The situation was bad indeed, but overlooking this truth and boasting of his ability to manage complicated affairs alone, Napoleon one day said to Talleyrand, "They have all been caught in the nets I spread for them, and I am now master of the situation in Spain as in the rest of Europe."

Talleyrand knew that Napoleon was lying. He knew that the Spanish people looked upon the French invaders with icy contempt and that England, to whom they had appealed, had already made some landings in Portugal and Spain and was trying to form a coalition of enemies of France in Europe. He knew also that Prussia and Austria, who had been waiting for a chance to avenge the Peace of Pressburg, were arming and that Alexander was wavering in his loyalty to Napoleon.

In short, he knew that the first step toward Napoleon's downfall had been successfully accomplished.

14.

The Betrayal at Erfurt

❧

Napoleon liked quick victories and so the situation in Spain was very distasteful to him. He, therefore, turned his attention to a grand and glamorous scheme which had long been brewing in the back of his mind, a scheme which involved the Czar of Russia.

Napoleon had met the Emperor Alexander fourteen months before at Tilsit when they signed the treaty following the battle of Friedland. He knew that Alexander had been impressed by him—admired him. Thirsting for more power and glory, Napoleon now hoped to develop a friendship with Alexander and explore a number of possibilities which had not been resolved at their last meeting. Upon their outcome would rest the destiny of Europe and the immortality of his name!

Friendship with Russia, Napoleon believed, would give him certain advantages he badly wanted. Russia could hold Austria in check for him, while he completely subdued Spain and drove England out of Portugal and Spain, banishing all British trade from the Continent. Russia was also the gateway to the Orient. If he could establish a firm friendship with

Alexander, the Czar would allow his armies to march through Russian territory, and he could take Constantinople and march on to India!

It was a grandiose scheme, one which did justice to the unbridled imagination and ambition of the Emperor of France, ruler of most of Europe, but it had a serious flaw. His new Minister of Foreign Affairs was not capable of handling the situation. In fact, there was only one man in all Europe equal to this diplomatic mission—Talleyrand. Besides, Talleyrand knew the Czar. They had met several times at Tilsit and had liked each other. In fact, the Czar had developed a deep respect for Talleyrand. And so although they were now separated by ill feeling, Napoleon was forced to call upon Talleyrand to advise him at a conference which he planned to hold at Erfurt, an old city in central Germany.

After revealing all his wishes to Talleyrand, Napoleon ended with these last instructions: "My dear Talleyrand, you must be at Erfurt a day or two before me. You know the Emperor Alexander well. You know how to speak to him. You will inform him of the benefit our alliance will prove to mankind."

Napoleon had used Talleyrand before. He would use him again and then . . . This was Napoleon's plan, but he was soon to learn that he had used Talleyrand once too often.

Napoleon was determined to make the conference at Erfurt a brilliant affair. "I wish to astonish Germany by my splendor," he said. But it wasn't only Germany he had in mind. He knew that the eyes of the civilized world would be on Erfurt and he wanted the world to behold a regal spectacle. He had his wish.

Several days before his arrival the flower-banked avenues and streets of the ancient little city began to bustle with crowds of elegant and important people arriving by carriage from every country of Europe. There were innumerable marshals, generals and other high officers in their most colorful uniforms, embroidered in gold and decorated with gleaming orders. There were noblemen and grandees, and dukes and princes and duchesses without number, all dressed in the finest silks and feathers and furs and accompanied by retinues of lackeys in livery. His German vassals were also present: the Kings of Bavaria, Saxony, Westphalia and Württemberg. Since he had expressed the wish that plays and other entertainments should be provided, there were also some of the most talented artists in Europe, including Talma, the great French actor.

Napoleon had expected the Czar to arrive in Erfurt before him. However, the Czar, jockeying for position, tarried on the way and so Napoleon arrived before him. This was his first disappointment. However, he took it in good spirits, and when he learned that Alexander was at last approaching, he went out to meet him on the road. "The two sovereigns rushed into each other's arms in a most friendly fashion," states a contemporary source. Then Napoleon returned to his apartments to await the Czar's official visit.

Talleyrand was present when Alexander entered, and when Napoleon presented him, the Czar said with a smile, "I am delighted to see him. I was hoping he would be here."

Later as Talleyrand was conducting him to his carriage, Alexander remarked, "We shall be seeing each other."

Returning to his lodgings, Talleyrand found a note from an old friend, the Princess of Thurn and Taxis, a sister of the Queen of Prussia. She had just arrived at Erfurt and was longing to see him.

Calling upon her that very evening Talleyrand was pleasantly surprised to meet the Czar for a second time. There was much pleasant talk and when tea was served the Czar suggested that it would be very nice if the Princess were to invite them to tea every evening. In this way, he said, they would have an opportunity to talk informally and end each day on an agreeable note.

Was this meeting accidental or had Alexander heard before he left for Erfurt that Napoleon's enemies had a "friend" in Paris? Could Talleyrand himself have contacted Alexander while he was still in Paris?

It doesn't matter much. What does matter is the fact that for the duration of the conference, Talleyrand and the Czar of all the Russias met almost every night at the apartment of the Princess of Thurn and Taxis.

On one of the first of these evenings, Talleyrand made his position crystal clear. He said, "Sire, it is in your power to save Europe, and you will only do so by refusing to give way to Napoleon. The French people are civilized; their sovereign is not. The Russian sovereign is civilized; his people are not. Therefore, the sovereign of Russia should be an ally of the French people." He then went on to explain that the natural borders of France were the Rhine, the Alps and the Pyrenees, and that the territory encompassed by these borders was all that the French people cared about. All the rest "is the Emperor's conquest and means nothing to France."

Thus assured of Talleyrand's sincerity, Alexander did not hesitate to report to him what exchange of ideas he had had with Napoleon each day. And from Talleyrand he received instructions on exactly how to behave on the following day. No one knew Napoleon better than Talleyrand. No one knew Napleon's plans better than Talleyrand, for he was also working each day with the Emperor. His advice to Alexander was

therefore so apt that the Czar sometimes made notes of his
actual words so that he could later voice them as his own.

It was a dangerous game Talleyrand was playing, an ugly
game. He was acting as adviser to one Emperor while deceiv-
ing the other, his own Emperor. It was a violation of all
faith and confidence. And Talleyrand knew the danger, for
the price of treason is death. Yet he was willing to risk all in
order to destroy Napoleon.

On the surface, everything appeared to be going well at
Erfurt. Each morning and afternoon Napoleon and Alexander met at the conference table. In the evenings there were
dinners, balls, concerts and theatrical performances. To please
Alexander, whose grandmother, Catherine the Great, had
been a patron and student of Voltaire's, Napoleon had several plays by this famous French historian, satirist and philosopher performed.

Everything was the essence of courtesy. The two Emperors
seemed to revel in each other's company. They complimented
each other at every opportunity. One evening when Voltaire's
Oedipus was being performed and the line was spoken, "The
friendship of a powerful man is a blessing from the gods,"
Alexander rose from his chair and grasped Napoleon's hand.
However, these public and private overtures led nowhere.
Alexander would not sign the treaty Napoleon placed before
him. He had many objections. He was obstinate.

Napoleon complained to Talleyrand. "I have thought it
over in all its aspects. . . . I have done nothing . . . he is just
narrowminded. I have not been able to get one step ahead."

When Talleyrand, trying to soothe Napoleon with flattery,
replied that the Russian Emperor was completely charmed
by him, Napoleon said very abruptly, "Well if he loves me
so much, why doesn't he sign?"

In the end, Napoleon reached an agreement with Alexander, but it was not the agreement he wanted. It was simply a renewal of the agreement they had signed before at Tilsit. It omitted all mention of Russia's holding Austria in check while Napoleon completed his subjugation of Spain and his strangulation of England. Talleyrand had stricken that clause from the document one evening while he and the Czar were drinking tea in the apartment of the Princess of Thurn and Taxis.

Napoleon's grand scheme had failed. He knew it only too well, but he was not to be stopped. He now presented a plan for uniting France and Russia through marriage. Late one night, after he was in bed, he called Talleyrand into his room.

"His agitation was most unusual," Talleyrand has recorded. "He asked me questions without waiting for an answer. He was trying to tell me something. He said what he didn't mean. At last he got out the great word—divorce." After all he was the founder of a dynasty and he had no heir. What would become of the throne of France? Alexander had a sister, the Grand Duchess Anna, who was of marriageable age. If she became his queen she could bear him an heir. Besides if she became his queen, France and Russia would be joined and together they would rule over all Europe.

Talleyrand promised to speak to Alexander about this most delicate subject, but once more he betrayed his Emperor. If Napoleon was going to divorce Josephine and marry a princess, then for the good of France and the peace of Europe, Talleyrand wanted her to be an Austrian princess. While speaking to Alexander as he had promised, Talleyrand made it clear that he did not approve of the proposal.

The Czar understood and was therefore quick to say that his sisters were ruled over by their mother, the Dowager Empress. She alone could grant permission for their marriage.

Napoleon considered this reply very reasonable. He believed that Alexander would influence the Dowager Empress in his favor and that the marriage would soon take place. He left Erfurt feeling that he had won. Alexander, who had made no concessions, felt he had won. Talleyrand also felt he had won.

He seems to have considered his role a noble one. He records in his *Memoirs* that his daily talks with Alexander were necessary for the welfare of Europe. "These conversations," he says, "put the Emperor in such a state of mind that the coaxing, the persuasion and the threats of Napoleon were of no use. . . ." Before leaving Erfurt "the Emperor Alexander was able to write in his own hand to the Emperor of Austria to reassure him" that no action would be taken against him.

Yes, Talleyrand felt that he had rendered Europe a great service at Erfurt. He summed it up by saying, "It was the last service I was able to render Europe, while Napoleon continued to reign. . . ." He went even further. Some years later he proclaimed, "At Erfurt, I saved Europe."

15.

Publicly Disgraced

✦

Events now ran on with reckless speed. The road was straight and the goal—disaster.

Napoleon left Erfurt and rushed to Spain where conditions needed his immediate attention. He ordered Talleyrand to go to Paris in the meantime and give some very large and lavish parties. He wanted Talleyrand to do this so that his supporters would have a chance to meet and exchange ideas. Talleyrand was instructed to report back everything that was said.

Talleyrand obeyed the Emperor's instructions. However, he also used these parties for his own purpose—to further Napoleon's fall. He went out of his way to make it clear to Paris that he disapproved completely of Napoleon's policy, and he encouraged the suspicions which were now whispered about that he was engaged with other discontented Frenchmen in planning to overthrow the Emperor. His tongue was sharp and he indulged in bitter criticism of the Spanish campaign and of Napoleon's other undertakings. He walked arm in arm through the salons with Fouché, the Minister of Police, a man whom everyone knew he had never been able to abide.

The situation was such that Metternich, the Austrian Ambassador to Paris, reported to his government that two parties now existed in France. "At the head of one of these parties is the Emperor . . ." he wrote. "At the head of the other party are "M. de Talleyrand, the Minister of Police and . . ."

Those who were devoted to Napoleon, and there were many in Paris as elsewhere in France, were horrified by what they saw and heard. As Talleyrand had expected they immediately notified Napoleon.

A clash was now inevitable. Talleyrand was ready. He repeated that phrase which had so often guided him, "Let time do its work."

Napoleon was at the point of successfully completing the conquest of Spain when the news of Talleyrand's treachery reached him. Had he stayed on, the course of future events would have been very different, but he considered it of the greatest importance to return at once to Paris. When he reached the Tuileries he immediately called a special meeting of the Privy Council, including several dignitaries of the Empire, which included Talleyrand and some Ministers of State such as Fouché.

After certain state affairs had been discussed and when everyone was ready to leave, Napoleon paused and, looking at those about him, expressed a note of displeasure. "Those whom I have made dignitaries or ministers cease to be free in their thoughts or in their expressions. They can only act through me. . . . For them, treachery begins when they allow themselves to have doubts; it is complete if they go from doubt to dissent."

There was a silence. Then the Emperor, impulsively and

nervously, walked toward Talleyrand who, because of his crippled foot, was leaning against a table, and burst into a violent tirade. "Thief!" he cried. "You are a thief! And you are a coward, a man of no faith. You do not even believe in God. All your life you have failed. You have failed in your duties. You have deceived and betrayed everyone. Nothing is sacred to you. Here I have showered you with riches, and there is nothing that you are not capable of doing against me. Thus for months, because you imagined things were going badly with me in Spain, you have been telling everyone that you advised me against this venture when in truth it was you who urged me into it. And about that unfortunate Duke d'Enghien, who informed me of his whereabouts? Who persuaded me to be cruel to him? So what are your designs? What do you want? What are you hoping for? Can you not speak out? You deserve to be broken, shattered like glass. I have the power to do it but I despise you too much to take the trouble. I should have had you hung. But there is still time."

He went on in a rage. Everyone present was terrified except Talleyrand, who all the time stood leaning against the table. He was silent. His face was paper white, his lips compressed, his only expression one of icy disdain.

Annoyed by his silence and contempt, Napoleon now tried to provoke his victim by making fun of his crippled foot and hurling insults at Mme. de Talleyrand, whom he had always disliked. But even this did not bring a response.

In complete desperation Napoleon finally cried out, "You are nothing but a silk stocking filled with dung!" He then stalked out of the room.

All eyes were fixed upon Talleyrand, who remained silent, seemingly unmoved. Then after a moment, he too walked out

of the room. Everyone followed. As they were passing down
the stairway he finally spoke. In a very matter of fact manner
he remarked to the man beside him, "What a pity that such
a great man should be so ill-bred!"

Those who had witnessed this terrible scene were certain
that it could mean only one thing—the end of Talleyrand.
However, Talleyrand added up all the charges that the Emperor had hurled against him. One was missing. The Emperor
had not yet heard of his betrayal at Erfurt. Napoleon did not
yet know the worst and so he was safe. He decided to continue in his usual manner, just as though nothing had happened.

That very evening he attended a party at the home of a
friend and regaled the guests with a more or less accurate
version of the frightful scene which had taken place. He
wanted Paris to hear the story from his own lips and he
wanted to show that he was not afraid.

The following day, he received a letter from the Emperor
depriving him of his position as Grand Chamberlain and
asking him to return the symbolic key of office. He wrote a
flattering reply designed to soften Napoleon's anger: "May
Your Majesty allow me to tell him . . . that for the first time
in my life I have obeyed him with sorrow. . . . I belong to
Your Majesty through the force of two feelings which no sorrow will be able to surmount nor weaken, gratitude and devotion which will end only with my life."

A few days later he startled everyone by appearing at a
function at court. He did not leave even after Napoleon had
ignored him completely by speaking to his two neighbors and
staring through him as though he did not exist. Knowing the
Emperor extremely well, he was sure that when his anger

cooled, he would regret his harsh words, and so he was willing to submit to still more public humiliation.

Two days later, he attended another court function. This time, when the Emperor spoke to his neighbors, Talleyrand quickly interrupted, answering a question the Emperor had asked. Then, before all assembled, he bowed and kissed the Emperor's hand.

Talleyrand had not miscalculated. Napoleon now began to soften. "I will do him no harm," Napoleon said to one of his associates a few weeks later. "I . . . have the same feelings for him that I had before. But . . . he will never have a private talk with me. He will no longer be able to say that he did or did not advise me to do one thing or another."

Napoleon foolishly thought that Talleyrand wanted to forget the insults he had hurled at him. He did not realize that Talleyrand would never forget and that he now burned so for revenge that he intensified all his treachery against him. He did not know that through his Uncle Alexander, Archbishop of Rheims, Talleyrand now began to correspond with Louis XVIII, brother of the beheaded Louis XVI, who was living in London. He did not know that, according to some historians, following the scene at the Privy Council, Talleyrand had entered into the service of the Austrian Emperor, who was waiting to avenge the Peace of Pressburg and was about to declare war against France. He did not know that Metternich had transferred 100,000 francs to Talleyrand as a first payment for services he was to render Austria!

War broke out between Austria and France early in 1809. It was a short war lasting only a few months, and Napoleon won. However, because of this war he lost prestige. He lost the battle of Aspern after two days of intense fighting, and everyone in Europe now took heart. Napoleon was not invincible!

This war, which cost Napoleon so much in status, would never have taken place except for Talleyrand. Had he not betrayed Napoleon at Erfurt, Alexander would have kept Austria in check. As it was, Alexander's most menacing action against Austria was to move his troops back and forth along his border. The defeat at Aspern might also never have occurred had Talleyrand not been turning over to Metternich secret plans and orders which he received daily from a spy at the front.

Yes, Napoleon had been fooled by Talleyrand into believing that he wanted to forget the insults which had been hurled against him. He misjudged Talleyrand. Many years later in the solitude of exile and when he knew all the facts, he confessed, "I made a great mistake. . . . I should either have imprisoned him or kept him always beside me. He could not escape the temptation to avenge himself."

However, all this Napoleon saw only after his complete defeat—after Waterloo.

16.

The Fall

❧

The Czar had never replied to Napoleon's proposal made at Erfurt, that he marry his sixteen-year-old sister, the Grand Duchess Anna. Napoleon had pressed the matter through the French Ambassador in St. Petersburg and the Russian Ambassador in Paris but had still received no answer. Never suspecting Talleyrand's duplicity in this matter, he felt deeply hurt. He thought that the Russian royal family did not consider him worthy of a Russian princess, and having finally divorced Josephine, he decided to seek the advice of his highest government officials. He called them together in January, 1810. Among them was Talleyrand, who still retained his position as Vice-Grand Elector!

Some felt that a Russian alliance was most desirable and advocated pressing St. Petersburg more firmly. Others favored a German alliance. Talleyrand, of course, spoke very eloquently for an Austrian alliance. In spite of two wars, he had still not given up hope of a Franco-Austrian pact. Besides he had the backing of Metternich and the newly divorced Josephine.

Metternich, who had just returned to Vienna and had been

made Foreign Secretary of Austria, was at that very moment consulting with his Emperor on this most important matter. With the utmost tact he was suggesting that a "family alliance" between France, the victor, and Austria, the vanquished, might be a most desirable political move. Therefore, why should not the Emperor present his lovely seventeen-year-old daughter, the Princess Marie Louise, to Napoleon as his bride?

Josephine was of the same opinion. She knew that the women of the House of Hapsburg were extremely fertile. Did not Maria Theresa, the mother of Marie Antoinette, have seventeen children! And so even though Napoleon had just divorced her, she said, "I am, and I shall remain, the Empress, but for nursery purposes he now needs someone else. I am going to do the selecting."

The result was that Napoleon married the young Austrian Princess, who had not even been consulted in the matter. As desired, she very soon bore a little son. Overjoyed, Napoleon at once crowned the infant, King of Rome.

Talleyrand now rested from his labors. He had often heard Napoleon say, "I follow the course of events; I have always marched with them." And Napoleon was now marching toward what Talleyrand was certain would be disaster.

Irritated by the Czar Alexander's "stubbornness" and obsessed with the desire to take India away from England, Napoleon had decided to invade Russia. Now that he did not have Talleyrand to check and disagree with every move he wanted to make, he was free to go ahead, and he did.

He raised and equipped the largest army Europe had ever seen. He mobilized a million men from France and his vassal states. In the spring of 1812, from a hundred points in Europe, they began marching eastward toward the Russian border.

The first battle did not occur until August 16 at Smolensk. At Borodino, about seventy-five miles west of Moscow, a second and very bloody battle was won. But it was not until September 15 that Napoleon reached Moscow.

Entering Moscow, Napoleon found the city completely deserted. Only a handful of people remained; everyone else had fled. There was no suitable place to garrison his army. He and his staff moved into the Kremlin, where he began dictating the terms of surrender to be signed by Alexander. But the Czar was nowhere to be found!

That night fires broke out in the city. Fanned by the wind, they spread from building to building. Four days later the city was a field of ashes. Then snow began to fall.

Day after day Napoleon waited impatiently in the Kremlin. But the Czar did not appear. His army, too, had disappeared far into the east.

Finally Napoleon, the conqueror, was forced to admit defeat. One bitter cold day, after a very heavy snowstorm, he gave the order to retreat, and his army, which he had intended to lead into India, started back for home across the frozen, windswept Russian steppes.

They straggled back, across the entire breadth of Europe, singly or in small groups, walking skeletons, their clothes in tatters and their feet wrapped in rags. One-third of the French army had been taken prisoners by the Russians, including forty-eight generals. The rest were killed or died of hunger and cold. Only one hundred thousand were fortunate enough to return home. Almost every family in France was in mourning.

Napoleon did not return with his troops. He deserted them

just as he had deserted his men in Egypt many years before. With only one companion he made a dash for Paris. He covered this great distance in the record time of 312 hours, or about 13 days!

He was pressed by the urgency of disaster. No longer was he "following the course of events." Events were now driving him.

Napoleon's military debacle in Russia gave courage to the nations of Europe. Prussia was the first to join the Czar. England and Sweden were next. Then Austria, whose Princess, Marie Louise, was on the throne of France, joined against Napoleon.

In his desperation Napoleon cried out, "If only I had Talleyrand! He could fix things up for me even now." And he appealed to Talleyrand. He even invited him to return to the Ministry of Foreign Affairs. But Talleyrand, who was pleased with the developments, seemed unconcerned. Knowing the ship was sinking, he had no intention of climbing aboard. Coldly he advised, "Negotiate while you still have something to negotiate with. . . . I am no longer acquainted with your affairs."

After all it was now four years since he had had the Emperor's confidence.

"You are trying to betray me," exclaimed the desperate Emperor.

"No," replied Talleyrand. "I will not assume office. The views I hold will add to the glory and happiness of France. Your views will not. We differ."

Napoleon did not wait for the allies to bring the war into France. He preferred to fight on foreign soil.

The first battle took place in the spring of 1813. The second and third battles were fought in August and the fourth battle was fought in October at Leipzig and is known as the Battle of the Nations. It lasted for three days and it was there that Napoleon met a defeat so crushing that he was unable to recover.

The allies now pushed him slowly back toward France. Finally growing weary of this, they decided to make a dash for Paris. Russia, Prussia and Austria pushed down from the north while Wellington, who had been fighting against the French in Spain, came up from the south.

Paris fell on the last day of March, 1814. Napoleon fled to his palace at Fontainebleau.

Talleyrand was in his home in Paris on that fateful day. As the allied troops marched into the city at eight o'clock the following morning, a friend came to see him. He was the Russian Ambassador, Nesselrode, and he had come "in the name of His Majesty."

Nesselrode explained that the Emperor Alexander had ordered him to come and show Talleyrand a draft of a proclamation to the people of Paris. Alexander wanted a Frenchman to speak to the French people in the language they understood.

While Talleyrand and Nesselrode were busy rewriting the proclamation, the Emperor Alexander arrived.

"Monsieur de Talleyrand," he said, "I have determined to stay in your house because you have my confidence and that of my allies. We do not wish to settle anything before we have heard from you. You know France, its needs and desires. Say what we ought to do and we will do it."

Talleyrand's hand could clearly be seen in the *Proclamation to the People of Paris* signed by the Czar Alexander and posted on buildings in all parts of the city.

In large clear type it announced that the "allied sovereigns" promised to "respect the wishes of the French nation." It also promised that the allies "will not treat with Napoleon Bonaparte nor with any member of his family" and that the Senate would be asked to "draw up a new constitution."

Reading it the people were impressed by its generosity and its promise of peace. Calm settled upon the city. In fact, the atmosphere was so relaxed that that evening the allied sovereigns all dined with Talleyrand and later went with him to the opera.

When Talleyrand entered the royal box accompanied by two emperors and a king, the whole house burst into cheers.

A virtual prisoner at Fontainebleau, Napoleon tried to negotiate with his enemies. He sent an aide to Alexander suggesting that he abdicate in favor of his little son, the King of Rome. The Czar hesitated. He knew that it would please the Austrian Emperor to have his little grandson on the French throne. But Talleyrand was set against it. He pointed out that, with a regency, Napoleon would in effect be ruler and that within a year he would be back in power and his armies would again menace Europe. All that had been gained would be lost. Alexander's answer to Napoleon was, "No."

Therefore, in the morning Napoleon signed his unconditional abdication. Then after delivering a very moving farewell address to a company of his faithful Old Guard, he got into the carriage which was to take him to a port in southern France where a vessel was waiting to carry him to Elba, his island of exile off the Italian coast. Talleyrand was disturbed. He said Elba was too close to France; he wanted Napoleon to be sent to the Azores.

Napoleon's great empire now lay in ruins. Tomorrow Talleyrand would begin rebuilding France.

17.

The Restoration

❦

The Czar Alexander was sincerely anxious to please the people of France. He wanted them to have the ruler of their choice. He thought of replacing Napoleon with some capable French statesman or military leader, but since he depended completely upon Talleyrand he did not press any of his ideas. Since Talleyrand still believed that a constitutional monarchy was the finest form of government and wanted it for France, he decided that the new ruler of France was to be the brother of the beheaded king, Louis XVI. He decided that the Bourbons must be re-established and that Louis XVIII must mount the throne.

"Our action must be based on principle," he said. "Louis XVIII is a principle. He is the legitimate King of France."

Alexander and his allies, the Emperor of Austria, the King of Prussia and the British government, agreed. All they asked was to see an end to revolutionary governments and upstart emperors in France. All they asked was that France should have a respectable and legitimate king upon the throne. And they agreed that France could have no better king than Louis XVIII of the House of Bourbon.

With this question settled and with the permission of Alexander and his allies, Talleyrand now took upon himself the task of pulling together the fragments of the shattered French government. Using his authority as Vice-Grand Elector, he summoned a meeting of the Senate.

Many senators had fled Paris before the invaders and so he was unable to gather a majority. But that did not stop him. He at once proposed that a provisional government of five be established, and he easily arranged to be named head of this all important committee.

The stage was now set for the recall of the Bourbon King. But there were two important matters Talleyrand first wanted to settle; they concerned the constitution and the flag.

Talleyrand was determined that the new government should be a constitutional monarchy just like the British government. He was determined to fulfill his dream. He brought out the constitution which had been drawn up by the National Assembly twenty years before and had it drastically revised to suit the situation. It had to be democratic enough to please the people and conservative enough to please the King. But above all, it had to provide for a Parliament like England's with two houses; a House of Nobles or Lords and a House of Commons.

He then turned his attention to the flag. Would the restoration of the Bourbons mean the return of the flag of the Bourbons, a white flag with gold Fleur de Lis, or would France retain the tricolor born of the Revolution? There were some senators who felt that the King would not accept the tricolor, but Talleyrand insisted that the tricolor must stay. He pointed out that the tricolor was the flag that had brought glory to France for the past twenty years, that it was the flag that the people loved.

Talleyrand had worked with amazing speed. He had organized a provisional government and settled the question of the constitution, the King and the flag in two short days! He now plunged into the task of working out the armistice and peace. He wanted to have it all settled before Louis XVIII returned to France. Once more he worked with unbelievable speed. He began the discussions for the armistice on the nineteenth and signed the terms on the twenty-third, just five days.

Since the opening days of his political career, Talleyrand had dreamed of only one thing—a stable moderate government for France and peace for Europe. His attempts had always been frustrated. This time, having a completely free hand, he was determined to realize his wishes.

Two years before, in 1812, France had held all of continental Europe from the coast of Spain to the Niemen and from Naples to Hamburg. Talleyrand sincerely felt that now the only way to lasting peace was for France to have a "legitimate king" and to control only her "legitimate lands." He denounced the "right of conquest." And on April 23, to the amazement of the Allies, who would have granted him many concessions, he signed the armistice which was later accepted and signed by Louis XVIII as the Treaty of Paris, giving up France's "natural boundaries" and all territories conquered by France during the Revolution and under Napoleon.

Talleyrand felt that giving up all conquered territory was the only way for France to overcome Europe's distrust and win back her confidence. It was the only way for France to return to a "policy of wisdom."

Louis XVIII, the fat fifty-eight-year-old Bourbon, entered Paris on May 2, 1814, and mounted the throne.

He was a fairly well educated man, but at times displayed the obstinacy and stupidity of an ignorant man. On being presented to the Senate by Talleyrand, he immediately displayed these damaging traits. He rose and said that while he did not object to a constitution, he demanded that it should be looked upon as an act of grace from the throne and not as one of the "rights" of the people. In short, he wanted to forget that history had been made during the last twenty years. He wanted to forget the Revolution, which was so dear to the hearts of the people, and he wanted to grant the people something they had forged for themselves and defended with their very blood!

No wonder a popular saying arose stating, "The stupidity of the Bourbons is so great that they never forget anything nor do events ever teach them anything." No wonder a cartoon appeared the next day in a newspaper picturing him as a fat pig. No wonder this cartoon caught the people's imagination and that from that moment on he was referred to as "Louis the Pig."

Louis XVIII had not made an auspicious beginning. However, it was the opinion of all clear-thinking men that in restoring the Bourbons, Talleyrand had done the wisest thing which could have been done at that critical historical moment. It was also the opinion of all that he had displayed great brilliance and foresight in the manner in which he had handled the situation.

He had acted with directness and singleness of purpose and had used moderation at all times. The whole thing had been accomplished without bloodshed and cruel arrests and imprisonments. And he had sought no post in the new government.

And so it came to pass that between the years 1789 and 1814 a full historical cycle had been accomplished. It had started with the Bourbon monarchy of Louis XVI and had been followed by the Revolution, the Directory, the Consulate, the Empire and the provisional government. It now returned again to the Bourbon monarchy.

These had been violent years and Talleyrand had played a part in each of these governments. No other political figure in France had survived all these changes. In fact, no statesman in all history has survived so many political changes.

Louis XVIII, not insensible to the services Talleyrand had rendered France and himself, rewarded Talleyrand by making him his Grand Chamberlain and by conferring on him the title of Prince de Talleyrand. This pleased Talleyrand very much. And from that day on he is known in history as Prince Talleyrand, for while he never used the Italian title of Prince which Napoleon had given him, he proudly used this French title which Louis now bestowed upon him.

However, these were not the only honors which Talleyrand received from his King. He was immediately appointed as Minister of Foreign Affairs to the new monarchy. The allies were planning to hold a congress in Vienna of all the nations of Europe in order to redistribute Napoleon's empire, and Louis XVIII wanted Talleyrand to represent France.

It was obvious to all, even the King, that no man in all France was better equipped to represent France, defeated, before her enemies.

For these negotiations Talleyrand would have to call into play all his political knowledge, his tact, his shrewdness, his diabolical craftiness, his gentle art of persuasion and his audacity. He was now standing on the threshold of his greatest achievement. He was sixty years old.

18.

The Congress of Vienna

❧

Never had such a glittering array of nobles assembled in Europe as during the Congress of Vienna. There were two emperors and their empresses, four kings, one queen, two heirs apparent, two grand duchesses, innumerable princes and princesses, dukes and duchesses and counts and countesses. There were court chamberlains, royal children, and titled ambassadors without number, and an army of servants wearing the liveries of every great house in Europe. Added to these were the marshals and generals of all the armies of Europe, distinguished statesmen, famous actors and a host of beautiful and adventurous women and handsome men, drawn to Vienna as by a magnate.

A few, like Talleyrand, had come to work, but most had come for the pomp, for the pageantry, for the social whirl. With Napoleon in exile and the Bourbons restored in France, they had come to celebrate the end of revolution and war. These nobles, who had never worked a day in their lives, had come to Vienna for a round of merriment.

There was no end to the banquets, balls, theatrical performances and concerts. The Austrian Emperor allowed the

great Beethoven, personally, to invite the crown heads of
Europe to a concert of his music. While they all attended,
they derived more pleasure from the many hunting parties,
shooting contests and the great mock tournament that was
staged to display the glory of their ancestors. Some of the
princes used medieval armor which they had brought with
them from their castles.

The ladies enjoyed the dances and masked balls best of all.
They thought it great fun to dance with a masked gentleman
and then discover at the end of the evening that he was a
king or famous duke.

And so it was in an atmosphere of frivolity that the Congress met week after week. Needless to say, very little work
was done. Because of this a saying became current, "The
Congress accomplishes nothing; but the Congress dances."

Outwardly nothing was to be seen but joyousness and glittering splendor. However, beneath this beguiling brightness
lay a dark and ugly side. One political intrigue upon another
developed. And to keep informed of everyone's most secret
plans, the Emperor of Austria, who was host, employed a
whole army of spies. Every coachman assigned to the visiting
royalty was a spy. Every butler and maid reported daily to the
Austrian secret police. The contents of every wastebasket
were collected each day and sent to a special place where they
were carefully examined. Every torn letter was pieced together and read. It is said that during the Congress of Vienna,
the Emperor of Austria employed one thousand spies!

Talleyrand came to Vienna in a most serious frame of
mind. He knew that his task would be very complicated and
would demand every ounce of his ability. However, he decided to make his establishment in Vienna as agreeable as
possible; a little entertaining was always helpful to diplo-

macy. He, therefore, asked his nephew's wife, the charming Dorothea, Countess Edmond de Périgord, to accompany him and act as his hostess—Talleyrand and his wife were separated.

Dorothea was one of the richest heiresses in Europe. The Czar Alexander and Talleyrand had arranged her marriage. Although she was only twenty-one, she was extremely well educated, speaking four languages, and was besides tactful, witty and had social grace, all so important in the world of diplomacy. Being an aristocrat, and both Russian and German by birth, and having spent the four years since her marriage in Paris, she knew everyone in the world of affairs and was, therefore, eminently well prepared to receive all Europe.

And so accompanied by Dorothea and bringing with him his secretaries, his chef and other servants, Talleyrand took a great mansion in Vienna. Within one week after his arrival everyone was speaking of the glamorous luxury of his receptions and of his gracious hospitality.

Talleyrand had arrived in Vienna several weeks before the opening of the Congress. He soon discovered that the representatives of the four great powers—Russia, Austria, England and Prussia—had already been meeting, in secret, and were dividing up Europe to suit themselves. They had decided that since France was the defeated nation she need not be consulted. Russia was particularly eager to gain a foothold in western Europe.

Talleyrand was not surprised. He had expected that the four powers would do just that. He did not complain or ask for an explanation. Nor did he humble himself with an appeal. Determined that France should be treated as an equal and that she should have a voice in remaking Europe, he went about gaining recognition for her in a most ingenious way.

He gathered together all the smaller nations of Europe which had been brushed aside by the big four and informed them of just what Russia, Austria, England and Prussia were planning to do with Europe, and he assured them of France's support. The result of this cunning move was that the big four suddenly awoke to find that defeated France was surrounded by friends and could no longer be ignored!

Talleyrand was immediately summoned to the "secret" meetings. He was prepared. He was deliberately curt and audacious. Although France was defeated he was not going to be humble.

As he entered the room and took the chair which had been provided for him, Castlereagh, the English Minister, said, "The object of today's meeting is to acquaint you with what the four powers have done since they have been here." Castlereagh then asked Metternich, who represented Austria and presided over the Congress, for the minutes of the secret meetings, which he passed to Talleyrand.

Talleyrand's eye immediately fell upon the words "allied powers." He stopped, pretending to be greatly surprised.

"Allied! Allied against whom?" he asked. "It is no longer against Napoleon; he is exiled and on the isle of Elba. It is no longer against France; the peace has been signed. It is surely not against the King of France; he guarantees the peace. . . . Gentlemen, let us speak frankly. If there are still allied powers, I am in the way here. . . . And yet if I were not here, you would miss me. I am perhaps the only one who is asking for nothing. Respect, that is all I ask for France."

His voice was strong, his manner profound. With his cane he now and again tapped the iron brace on his leg giving accent where he felt it was needed. No smile dispelled the seriousness of his expression.

He continued, "The presence of a minister of Louis XVIII consecrates the principle on which all social order is based. Europe's chief need is to banish forever the notion that rights may be won by conquests and return to the sacred order of Legitimacy."

There was a deep silence. All were astonished by his boldness but impressed by his reasoning. Embarrassed at having tried to exclude France, they now tried to explain that the term "allied powers" had been used only "for the convenience and brevity."

"Brevity cannot be purchased at the expense of accuracy!" Talleyrand answered sharply.

Then again picking up the minutes of the secret meetings, he glanced over the contents. "For me there are only two dates, the thirtieth of May when it was agreed to hold a Congress and the first of October when the Congress is to open. As far as I am concerned nothing has taken place between them."

The ministers of the four powers were now on the defensive. They said that since little or nothing had been accomplished at their secret meetings, they were prepared to withdraw the minutes of their work.

Talleyrand's only reply was that since he considered all their previous meetings null and void, he wanted the minutes of these meetings to be destroyed. He insisted that they be destroyed. And they were.

On the following day, Talleyrand presented the four powers with a note stating that the eight powers which had signed the Treaty of Paris were the only ones qualified to draw up the "order of business" for the Congress. In this way he got Portugal and Sweden, two of the little countries which he had befriended just two days before, to have a voice in the pro-

ceedings. But he was still not satisfied. He wanted all the little
powers to have a voice in the deliberations of the Congress;
he rightly claimed that only then would the Congress be
truly representative, only then could the Congress solve
Europe's problems and bring about a lasting peace. Besides,
having won the friendship of the little nations, he now
wanted to use them for his own benefit. When he became
locked in a battle against the four great powers, their voice
would help him win his point.

Day after day Talleyrand continued with his bold and calculated moves. He knew the men with whom he was dealing.
He had negotiated with them before at other conferences. He
also knew that with the exception of England each one of
them had at one time or another courted Napoleon's favor.
Had not the King of Prussia once promised to give Napoleon
troops for further conquests? Had not the Czar of all the
Russias openly expressed great admiration for Napoleon and
entered into alliances with him at Tilsit and Erfurt? And the
Austrian Emperor, had he not willingly given Napoleon one
of his daughters in marriage?

"Who is the guilty one?" he asked. "Certainly not France.
And not the French King." There was an edge of irony in
his voice.

In this way, pointing the finger of guilt and with audacity,
with bold facts that were undeniable and with a knowledge
of all the secret treaties which had been made in Europe during the past twenty years, Talleyrand defied the ministers of
the four great powers. And all the while, he kept repeating
these words, as though they were a refrain, "France wants
nothing."

It was a brilliant performance. As a result and before the
Congress was officially opened, it was agreed that defeated

France should be put on an equal footing with the four great powers which had conquered her! The four great powers were now five: England, Austria, Russia, Prussia and France.

Talleyrand had won a tremendous victory for France. He knew that as the Congress progressed, England, Russia, Austria and Prussia would quarrel over different problems which would arise. He also knew that the sovereigns of Austria, Prussia and Russia, who were making a public show of friendship, really hated each other. And so when their votes would be divided two against two, it would be his vote for France which would serve as the deciding factor.

In other words, it would be defeated France who would control the destiny of Europe!

The Congress of Vienna opened officially on November 1, 1815. From the very first session it was Talleyrand who dominated all the proceedings by his skillful diplomacy.

His first move was to establish his theory of "Legitimacy" as the basis for all discussions. This meant that the territories and the royal houses which existed in Europe before the Revolution should be restored wherever possible. Keeping this always in mind, he then maneuvered the representatives through the thorny problems which confronted them.

The meetings were many and charged with tensions. At one point Russia and Austria became so embroiled that war threatened. But in the end, solutions were found for all difficulties.

In brief, the results were as follows: Ferdinand was confirmed as ruler of Spain; Poland was divided between Russia, Austria and Prussia; Holland and Belgium were united into the kingdom of the Netherlands; a Confederation of German States was created; Switzerland was enlarged; Prussia got West Pomerania, parts of Saxony, Westphalia and the

Rhine Province; England retained Ceylon, the Cape Colony in South Africa, Malta and Helgoland and got from the Netherlands and Spain some valuable islands in the West Indies; and Italy was once more divided into different duchies and kingdoms, a number of which were restored to Austria.

Talleyrand was pleased with the way the Congress was going. He felt that his efforts would bring peace to Europe. He had increased his personal wealth—the King of Saxony alone gave him 6,000,000 francs for his aid. However, what pleased him most was that he had thwarted Russia's designs in western Europe and had by the beginning of January, 1815, broken up the coalition between the enemies of France: Russia, Prussia, Austria and England. He had accomplished more than this, much more. He had realized his old dream of gaining Austria and England as allies of France, and on January 3, an alliance of friendship and mutual aid had been signed between France, England and Austria.

The three strongest nations of Europe were now friends and would ensure the peace. "France is no longer isolated in Europe," Talleyrand wrote with great satisfaction to Louis XVIII.

Talleyrand was extremely pleased with the alliance. But suddenly, that which he had worked so long to attain, became a meaningless scrap of paper and England and Austria abandoned France and rejoined their old allies, Russia and Prussia. Suddenly the dancing in Vienna stopped. Couriers on horseback reached the city with shattering news from France. Napoleon, "the scourge of Europe," had escaped from Elba with his personal guard of eight hundred men and had landed near Cannes on the southern coast of France!

The Congress was dumbfounded by the news and the dispatches which reached Vienna during the following week only increased the bewilderment. They stated that heading toward Paris, Napoleon was acclaimed everywhere. Men old and young left their homes to march once more under his Eagles. At Grenoble the King's garrison enthusiastically joined his ranks. Lyons surrendered without a shot. His numbers increased to 14,000 then to 20,000. Marshal Ney and his troops, whom the King sent to stop Napoleon's advance, also joined him. The frightened King now fled to Belgium, and Napoleon entered Paris without a shot being fired and once more mounted the throne of France!

Talleyrand was one of the very few at Vienna who was not rendered incapable of action by the news. Instantly realizing what a difficult position he, Louis XVIII and France had been thrown into by the sudden turn of events, he tried by every means to prove to Europe that France and her "legitimate" government were in no way to blame. He reminded everyone that he had opposed Elba as the place of exile. "I proposed the Azores . . . they are five hundred miles to any land," he said.

He then arranged that France and the other powers which had signed the Treaty of Paris condemn Napoleon. He drew up a document which read: "The Powers declare that Napoleon Bonaparte is outlawed from social and civil relations and that, as the enemy and disturber of the peace of the world, he has laid himself open to public prosecution." He then pledged Louis XVIII and France as members of the coalition which was immediately formed to oppose Napoleon.

19.

Talleyrand Returns to Paris

❧

The Congress of Vienna closed on June 9, 1815, and Talleyrand, his work completed, hurried to join Louis XVIII in Belgium near Ghent where he had taken refuge. Talleyrand was very irritated that the King had fled from Paris and abandoned France, and had surrounded himself in Belgium with a group of Royalist émigrés, who hated everything about the Revolution and wanted to erase every trace of it and return to the past.

While still in Vienna, Talleyrand had sent the King a long report warning him against associating with such people, listing the great number of mistakes His Majesty had made during the past year because of heeding the advice of Royalists. His report was critical but also constructive, for it suggested a number of remedies.

Realizing that Napoleon could never have made such a triumphant return to France if the people had been satisfied with the restored monarchy, and admitting that the constitution which he had drawn up so hurriedly the year before was not perfect, Talleyrand advised the King to revise it on more democratic lines. He also advised the King to form a new

government before returning to France. And he warned him
against taking any of his Royalist friends into the government. These people he said had lived abroad for twenty years
and were completely out of touch with France. France had
gone through the agony of the Revolution to free itself from
feudal bondage. It had endured an Empire which had cost
millions of lives to satisfy the burning ambition of Napoleon.
Public opinion could not be thrown to the winds. The people
must be given the kind of government they wanted, a government which guaranteed the rights of man; otherwise they
would return to Revolution.

On his way to Ghent on June 19, Talleyrand learned that
Napoleon had been completely defeated by the allies at the
battle of Waterloo and that again, as in Egypt and Russia, he
had deserted his army and rushed back to Paris.

Arriving at Brussels shortly afterward, he learned that
Louis XVIII had left Ghent and was following the allied
armies into France. He was at that moment in the city of
Mons not far from the French border. Talleyrand hurried to
find him there, but his heart was heavy, for he knew that his
meeting with Louis would not be an easy one because of the
letter which he had sent him from Vienna. He knew that
Louis was very sensitive to criticism and that under the influence of his Royalist friends would greet him coolly if at all.
And he was right.

Reaching Mons, Talleyrand found that the King was already in his coach and ready to leave the city. To show his
displeasure, he did not even get out of his coach to greet the
man who had restored him to the throne of France and who
had served him and France with such brilliance and devotion
at the Congress of Vienna. Sitting in his great coach he let
Talleyrand stand at its side while he spoke to him!

The insult went beyond all bounds, but Talleyrand was determined to show the King that he was not cowed and would not be brushed off so easily. He handed him another "letter of advice," which he had prepared while traveling from Vienna to Belgium, stating his opinions in the clearest terms.

Again he criticized the manner in which the King had behaved and governed since coming to the throne, saying that while "Legitimacy" was triumphing at Vienna, it was being undermined at home by those who confused Legitimacy with Absolutism, that dead principle of the Divine Right of Kings. In the letter he stated, "The spirit of the times in which we live demands that in great civilized states supreme power shall only be exercised with the consent of bodies drawn from the heart of the society that it governs."

He went on to say that liberty of the individual, freedom of the press, which Louis had tried to curb, and an independent system of judiciary must be guaranteed the people. And he warned Louis that these views were not peculiar to France but were, as he had discovered in Vienna, held by people all over Europe. The ideals of the French Revolution had been adopted by the people in many lands.

The King could easily have asked for Talleyrand's resignation. He had never liked Talleyrand, and although he owed him his throne, he felt no gratitude. However, he still needed him. He recognized his genius and felt that no one else could handle the uncertain opening months of his second restoration. And so back in Paris he at once appointed him to two posts in the new government. He made him Minister of Foreign Affairs and President of the Council of Ministers, or Prime Minister.

As Prime Minister it was Talleyrand's duty to form a cabinet and conclude a new peace with the allies who had just defeated Napoleon for a second time. He gathered about him a cabinet of able men, but they were not equal to the difficult situation which confronted them.

Talleyrand had hoped at Vienna that by aligning France with Russia, England, Austria and Prussia in their coalition to fight Napoleon, France would escape a harsh peace after the victory. But he was mistaken.

England was the only country which wanted to deal kindly with France after Waterloo. General Blücher, the Prussian, felt otherwise and he prevailed upon the allies to deal with France as with a criminal and punish her to the fullest.

The allies first demanded that the French Army be disbanded. With France "bound hand and foot," the allies then began a brutal occupation. The French were forced to pay 1,750,000 francs a day for the maintenance of the allied troops, who committed the most dreadful excesses against the French in all parts of the country. The situation was so bad that Talleyrand feared a national uprising. He warned the allies and pleaded with them, but little was done to alleviate the dreadful conditions.

Talleyrand fared no better at the peace negotiations. The allied treaty demanded that France surrender eight cities and forts along her borders, and the departments of Mont Blanc and Savoy, and that she pay an indemnity of 600,000,000 francs plus 200,000,000 for the construction of a line of fortresses along the French border to imprison her within. It further demanded that France support 150,000 allied soldiers who were to occupy twelve sections of the French border, for a period of from three to seven years.

Talleyrand tried every means to have these excessively harsh terms softened. He pointed out that since, in Vienna,

France had joined the allies, she should not now be treated as
an enemy. The coalition had been formed to fight Napoleon,
not Louis XVIII and the legitimate French government
which was once more in command in France. "To demand
concessions," he said, "there has to be a conquest." But the
allies would not listen. They stood firm. Talleyrand was
finally forced to sign the brutal document.

Taking advantage of this "failure," Talleyrand's enemies
now attacked him in the most vicious way, saying among
other things that he had not defended France to the fullest of
his abilities. It became clearer each day that he could not
survive unless given a vote of confidence by the King. And so
he appeared before Louis XVIII.

The King listened politely while Talleyrand defended his
actions. But when he spoke the words, "Unless Your Majesty
guarantees us his formal support . . . we ask the King this very
day to choose new counselors" the King interrupted him and
said very coldly, "Well, then, I shall take another Minister."

The rejection was complete. Talleyrand had to resign both
his posts as Minister of Foreign Affairs and as Prime Minister.
He was bitterly wounded but tried to speak of it in a joking
manner.

"We are leaving without any compliments," he wrote to
one of his friends. "The ingratitude is not disguised enough."
And to another friend he remarked, "The King seemed en-
chanted to get rid of us."

He had been Prime Minister and Minister of Foreign Affairs for the reinstated government exactly ten weeks. "I have
spent thirty years of my life thinking of nothing except what
could be useful to my country," he wrote with a note of bitterness. "Today I am busy with my own affairs."

It had been a hard and disappointing ten weeks. Except for

one thing, nothing had turned out as Talleyrand wished. The allies had banished Napoleon to the distant island of St. Helena off the coast of Africa. There on that rocky mound Napoleon was doomed to spend the rest of his days. His destruction was now complete.

20.

Three Kings

❧

Talleyrand's great wealth allowed him to enjoy his retirement. He was able to entertain in the same lavish manner as he had while serving the government, and because he was so well known both at home and abroad, his mansion in Paris and his château at Valençay were always filled with the most interesting and important people of Europe.

However, after only three or four months and in spite of the fact that he was sixty-two years old, he began to weary of his idleness and longed to re-enter the political scene. So he took his seat in the upper house, to which he was entitled because of his noble birth, and soon became one of the leaders of the opposition, repeatedly casting his vote in defense of the freedom of the press and other liberties won by the people during the Revolution, which the King and his government now wanted to abolish.

The government was in the hands of ultraconservative men. Among other things they advocated censorship of the press, and they gave military aid to King Ferdinand of Spain to impose an absolute monarchy upon the Spanish people.

Warning the King and his ministers and other supporters,

Talleyrand said that one could not survive against the needs of the time. He said that the Revolution was in accord with the time when it proclaimed religious liberty, equality, trial by jury and freedom of the press. These rights of man were still in accord with the age, and to try to deny them would only lead to disaster.

His words were charged with reason, but it did no good, because Louis, being a Bourbon, was incapable of learning. So he continued in his reckless and destructive way. The gulf between Talleyrand and the "legitimate" King, whom he had restored, grew wider each day. To make his opposition more forceful, Talleyrand, who had always been a moderate, even a conservative, now joined the liberals in the Senate, and his home in Paris became their meeting place. In fact, he became such a gadfly to the ultraconservatives who were friends of the King and who controlled the government that the King wanted to get rid of him.

"Aren't you planning to go live in the country, Prince?" the King asked him one day.

Talleyrand continued his opposition to the King's government for the first several years of his retirement. But it was not the sort of politics for which he was best suited. He had always played upon a large stage and with the most important historical characters. He longed for the power he had once wielded. And so he was not happy.

Besides, he was growing older. He was now over sixty-five and the ranks of his devoted friends were being thinned out by death. It was at this time that a childhood friend died. "Of the people with whom I was brought up he was the last," Talleyrand wrote sadly. "Of that generation I remain the only survivor."

Shortly after this, he learned of the death of his beloved

and most faithful friend, Madame de Staël, and not long after, he lost his friend the Duchess de Courland, Dorothea's mother. They had been most devoted to each other and she had continued writing to him until her very last days. These deaths were followed by that of his Uncle Alexander, who had once been Archbishop of Rheims and who, after the Restoration, had been elevated by Louis XVIII to Cardinal and Archbishop of Paris.

In the same year, 1821, he learned that Napoleon had died on St. Helena. The news came to him while he was attending a dinner at the home of a friend. Wellington was one of the guests. No one was surprised, for it had been known for some time that Napoleon was suffering from cancer. Still when the announcement was made a hush fell over the room.

"What an event!" exclaimed the hostess, breaking the si. lence.

"Event!" said Talleyrand. "A cannonball, a few years ago, would have put a better end to this extraordinary life. . . . It is no longer an event. It is only a piece of news."

Three years later it was the fat and stupid Bourbon, Louis XVIII, who was called to his grave. He was buried with the ancient pomp given the feudal Kings of France.

After the coffin was placed in the tomb, four dukes covered it with the colors of the four companies of the Guard. Then the crown, the scepter and the hand of justice were placed upon it. After this the spurs, breastplate, sword, shield and gauntlets worn by French kings in battle—but never worn by Louis, who had always run away—were put upon the coffin.

Then came the last rite of homage. Talleyrand, the aged Grand Chamberlain, the one whom the ungrateful King had dismissed so rudely and who now regretted that he had placed

such a stupid Bourbon on the French throne, limped forward
and lowered the flag of France, the tricolor born in the days
of the Revolution, over all.

Having laid the King of France to rest with all the honors
and homage due a feudal monarch, Talleyrand now played
his part in the coronation of Louis' younger brother, Charles
X. For this ceremony he journeyed to Rheims.

How long ago it all seemed! Memories of the past rushed
one upon the other. Had he not as a youth once lived at the
cathedral of Rheims with his uncle? Was it not there that he
had taken his vows as a priest? And was it not there also at
the great Cathedral of Rheims that long ago, he had attended
the coronation of Louis XVI and Marie Antoinette. "We are
so young," the twenty-year-old Louis had whispered to his
eighteen-year-old Queen. "They have taught us nothing. May
God help us."

All these things had taken place forty years ago and more.
What a rushing torrent of history had ensued! Now another
Bourbon was mounting the throne of France, a Bourbon
whom Talleyrand feared was like his brother Louis and his
forefathers and had "never learned anything." Another Bourbon dedicated to restoring the dead past!

Philosophically Talleyrand remarked, "The more it
changes, the more it remains the same."

Talleyrand's fears concerning Charles X were justified. He
hated the Constitution and all the "rights" that had come to
the people of France through forty years of suffering. He
immediately surrounded himself with reckless extremists of
the far right, deeply dyed Royalists, who at once engaged in a
war with all the liberal and moderate forces in the government.

Charles X, and his government, was so reckless that among

other things he wanted to compensate all émigrés for their
lost property, and he had his Prime Minister present a bill in
the Senate stating that nothing could be printed in France
unless it had been submitted five days before to the government for approval.

"It is not French, because it is stupid," said Talleyrand in
protest. Realizing that Charles X was an even poorer ruler
than Louis XVIII, he decided that he must be overthrown.
Although Talleyrand was now seventy-five years old he un-
dertook the task himself.

The first move he made was to pick a successor to Charles X.
He decided upon Louis-Philippe, Duke of Orleans, a member
of the liberal faction and son of Louis-Philippe Joseph, the
Red Prince, one of the few noblemen who had voted for the
execution of Louis XVI.

Talleyrand's next move was to associate himself with two
young and very able writers named Thiers and Carrel, who
were also deeply troubled by the King's complete inability
as a ruler. He gave these young men money to establish a
paper called the *National,* dedicated to destroying the government.

The first issue appeared in January, 1830, and for the next
seven months its attacks against the ultraconservative government were relentless. With each issue the paper gained more
and more readers. And it is true that the government unin-
tentionally helped, by dissolving the newly elected Senate and
interfering with free elections!

Tension mounted. Sensing that there might be serious
trouble ahead, the King said to Talleyrand, "A king who is
threatened with revolution has no choice. It is either the
throne or the scaffold."

"Sire, Your Majesty forgets the post chaise," replied Talleyrand.

Finally, on July 28 the storm broke. The Ministry, hoping to silence all opposition, and especially the *National,* abolished completely the freedom of the press. Revolution broke out in Paris. The people took up arms and swarmed out into the streets. They invaded the City Hall.

The next day Louis-Philippe entered Paris and Charles X fled in a post chaise just as Talleyrand had suggested.

Explaining his part in these stirring events, Talleyrand said, "We did not abandon the King. It was the King who abandoned us."

21.

Ambassador at the Court of St. James

❖

Talleyrand had preached the doctrine of Legitimacy at the Congress of Vienna. It had been adopted as the basis for all the negotiations. And since that time Russia, Austria and Prussia had abided strictly to this principle. Whenever and wherever men, inspired by the Liberty, Equality and Fraternity of the French Revolution, had tried to overthrow their oppressive governments Russia, Austria and Prussia had sent armed forces to impose Legitimacy.

There had been many such uprisings and the policing actions did not seem to stop them. The decade between 1820 and 1830 had been particularly bad.

England had taken no active part in these policing actions. Neither had France, but both had supported Legitimacy at home—that is, until Charles X was overthrown and the liberal Louis-Philippe was placed upon the French throne.

Russia, Austria and Prussia naturally looked upon the upheaval in France with the greatest of disapproval and distrust. Was France again going to pollute Europe with more revolutionary ideas? Was France again going to terrorize Europe with war? Would it not be best to invade France now and restore Legitimacy before things got completely out of hand? These were the questions Russia, Austria and Prussia asked themselves. To add to the seriousness of the situation, the July Revolution in Paris had inspired a revolt among the Belgians. Conditions were nearing the breaking point. War was imminent.

Talleyrand and Louis-Philippe were very conscious of the seriousness of the situation. Anxious to restore France to political respectability and gain a powerful friend for her, they decided to try to win England's support. After all, England and France had many things in common. Both lands had constitutional monarchies. In both lands liberty was respected. And both countries had free elections, a free press and freedom of speech, all of which was unique in the Europe of 1830. No other two countries were so far advanced. Besides, it had always been Talleyrand's dream to have a strong alliance between France and England. He had succeeded at the Congress of Vienna only to have all his work dashed to pieces by the return of Napoleon from Elba. Now, it was decided he should try again.

Therefore, after fifteen years of having been excluded from power, Talleyrand once more returned to the diplomatic arena. In spite of the fact that he was now seventy-six and badly troubled by his crippled foot, Louis-Philippe called him into service as Ambassador to St. James.

"It is not at Paris," Talleyrand explained to his friends, "it is at London that I am needed."

The guns at Dover saluted the arrival of the distinguished French Ambassador. How strange one's fate can be. After thirty-eight years he was returning to London on the same

mission on which the Revolutionary government had sent
him in 1792—to keep England from joining with France's
enemies on the Continent and to enter into an alliance with
England. He had failed that time. Now he was filled with
hope.

He was happy and flattered to hear the booming of the
welcoming salute at Dover. He was even more flattered by
the warm welcome he received on entering London. People,
seeing his carriage and hoping that his visit would prevent
war, stopped to wave to him. Gentlemen tipped their hats.
Some even cheered and shouted, "Hurrah for Louis-Philippe!"

Talleyrand had been cheered only once before, at the
Opera in Paris. He had never been cheered by strangers. He
was a bit embarrassed. However, sitting there in his carriage,
in a big coat with a great white muslin cravat hiding his chin
and with an enormous cockade, six inches square, on his hat
and a knot of ribbons pinned to his lapel, in the red, white
and blue of the Revolution, he managed to smile and wave.

Dorothea served Talleyrand as hostess here in London,
just as she had in Vienna and in Paris and Valençay. She
brought the servants with her, all wearing the Talleyrand-
Périgord livery: maids, butlers, lackeys, coachmen, even the
chef. Talleyrand often said that an ambassador's chef was
more important than a good secretary. Because of this and
the fact that Dorothea was by now one of the most accomplished of all diplomatic hostesses, the French embassy in
Hanover Square, with its enormous and luxurious drawing
room, became the center of London society.

Talleyrand's entertainments and dinners soon acquired a
reputation for unsurpassed elegance and splendor. There was
an ease and grace to his hospitality. And such food had never
before been served in London.

"Our dinners are a success," wrote Dorothea to a friend. "They are making history in London gastronomy. But it's ruinous." Even Talleyrand, who was accustomed to spending great sums of money, was a little concerned. However, knowing the value of this kind of entertaining, he said that the receptions, parties and dinners should continue on the same lavish scale.

And he was right. What he did not win at the diplomatic table he won at the dinner table. When he first arrived in London he found a most hostile attitude toward France and her new government at many of the embassies. The Russian embassy was almost warlike in its manner. But before a year was over a London newspaper commented, "Everyone here is at his feet. . . . All the nobility of England seek his society. The diplomats of every land bow before him."

The Duke of Wellington, hero of Waterloo, was Prime Minister of England. He and Talleyrand had been good friends for many years. Both had been enemies of Napoleon. Both had worked together at the Congress of Vienna and to establish peace after Waterloo. Now they were together again and once more trying to find a way to quiet European unrest. The first task confronting them was the most difficult. It concerned the Belgian revolt.

At the Congress of Vienna, Belgium and Holland had been incorporated into one nation under the rule of the King of Holland, the kingdom of the Netherlands. It had been expressly created to satisfy England, who wanted a strong nation to the north of France to prevent her from ever regaining control of the east coast of the Channel.

On August 25, 1830, just one month before Talleyrand left for London, the Belgians revolted and a pro-Belgian party immediately formed in France. These people called the Belgian revolt a sister of the July Revolution, and they demanded armed intervention in defense of the Belgians, saying that it would prove to all Europe that France was one with all those peoples who overthrew their oppressors. Such talk naturally alarmed every monarch in Europe. To make matters worse, a party now arose in Belgium asking either for a union with France or for one of Louis-Philippe's sons to be made King of Belgium.

Talleyrand had to act quickly. He was finally able to persuade Louis-Philippe and his Ministers to come out strongly against any intervention whatsoever.

In London, Talleyrand was now able to propose a principle for guiding Europe in the Belgian affair, the principle of nonintervention. He said that if England would persuade Russia, Austria and Prussia not to intervene in favor of the King of the Netherlands, France would promise not to take over Belgium either directly or indirectly.

It was a master stroke. Wellington quickly pledged England to nonintervention and agreed to press the advisability of this principle upon his allies: Russia, Austria and Prussia.

The matter was brought up that November at the Conference of London attended by these nations, and after much discussion and maneuvering, Talleyrand's principle of nonintervention was adopted. The result was that the kingdom of the Netherlands was dissolved and Belgium was declared an independent state. To prevent Holland from ever trying to retake her, to allay England's fears and to protect France from invasions from countries in the north, her neutrality was guaranteed by all.

Talleyrand had worked very closely with England during the entire Conference. He had managed everything extremely well. The result was that he inadvertently gained what he wanted most; during the long months of the Conference, England had learned that working closely with France was extremely beneficial to her. Together they created a political and military block which was almost impossible for the rest of Europe to challenge. And so England and France entered into an alliance, that alliance of mutual aid and understanding of which Talleyrand had dreamed all his life!

"From the beginning to the end of my career," Talleyrand wrote, "a close alliance between France and England has been my dearest wish, since I am convinced that world peace, the strengthening of liberal ideas, and the progress of true civilization can be furthered only by such an alliance."

He was satisfied. His work was now done. And so he returned to Paris and sent his letter of resignation to the Minister of Foreign Affairs. It was a triumphant return. The year was 1834. Talleyrand was eighty years old.

22.

The Final Years

❧

Talleyrand spent the last four years of his life between Paris and Valençay.

His beloved Dorothea stayed with him, caring for him with the greatest of tenderness. However, his life was neither easy nor pleasant. His years made him frail and to the discomfit of his lame foot was added the suffering of rheumatism. "I am not happy, I am not unhappy," he confided in his journal. "My health is not good, it is not bad. I am getting weaker very gradually."

His only real pleasure was his friends, who still flocked to see him and Dorothea and her little daughter, Pauline. He no longer enjoyed food and wine. He ate only one meal at the end of the day. And he never drank, except a little wine at this meal.

He began to develop imaginary fears. He feared that he might have a heart attack. To prevent this he had his bed hollowed out in the middle so that he could sleep in a sitting position. He also took to wearing several thick night-caps to protect his skull in case he should fall out of bed during the night! He was now so old, his face was so wrinkled and his hair so stringy, that someone remarked, "He looks like an old lion."

However, his mind was still clear. He made his will, leaving his great fortune to his nephews. But this was not all that his will contained. In it he made a very curious provision. It stated that while he never regretted the fact that he, almost singlehandedly, had been responsible for the destruction of Napoleon, one of the most powerful emperors in all history, still his sense of justice demanded that he record that he considered Napoleon as his benefactor. "For the fortune I am bequeathing my nephews comes in great part from him. Therefore, if ever a man bearing the name of Bonaparte should be in need it is their duty to assist him."

In March, 1837, he made his last public appearance. It was at the French Academy of Moral and Political Science, of which he was a member and which had been founded at his suggestion many, many years before by the Revolutionary government. The occasion was the funeral service for a friend and colleague, Count Karl Reinhard, who had succeeded him as Minister of Foreign Affairs under the Directory. Talleyrand asked to be allowed to deliver the funeral oration. "It will be my farewell to the public," he said.

His doctor warned that he would not be responsible for the consequences. To this Talleyrand replied with his usual spirit, "Who asked you to be responsible?"

All Paris crowded into the hall of the Academy for this historic event. When the ushers announced, "The Prince," everyone rose.

Supported by two ushers, Talleyrand entered slowly and made his way to the podium. He drew a sheaf of papers from his pocket and began to read in a clear, deep and resonant voice. He used no spectacles.

He began by reviewing the distinguished career of his friend and listing his great virtues. And it became apparent almost immediately that Talleyrand was speaking not just of Reinhard but also of himself, for there were certain similarities in their lives. As a young man Reinhard had also studied for the Church, and Talleyrand explained how this theological training had been of invaluable advantage.

He then went on to describe what qualities a perfect Minister of Foreign Affairs must possess: His instinct should prevent him from compromising himself in any conversation. He should appear open and still remain sealed. He should be able to mask his reserve with careless abandon. His conversation should be simple, varied, surprising, always neutral —sometimes even naïve. And during every moment of the twenty-four hours, he should remember that he is a Minister of Foreign Affairs.

Talleyrand then probed deeper. He went into the philosophy of statesmanship. "Yet all these qualities, rare as they are, may not suffice. Good faith is necessary to give them the guarantee which they usually require. . . . Diplomacy is not a science of deceit and duplicity. Good faith is necessary in all political transactions, for it is good faith that makes them firm and lasting. People have made the mistake of confusing reserve with deceit. Good faith never authorizes deceit, but it admits of reserve. And reserve has this peculiarity, that it increases confidence."

The audience was deeply impressed. They had been conducted on a personal tour behind the scenes and through the dark mysterious labyrinth of diplomacy. They had been taken there by the man who for more than half a century had dominated the political stage of Europe—the man who had made and broken mighty rulers. They were awed and mute with wonder as the old man left the hall supported by the two ushers.

Victor Cousin, a French philosopher and a member of the Academy, said with enthusiasm that Talleyrand's address was better than Voltaire. Higher praise was impossible. And this praise was shared by the Paris press.

Two months after this crowning success Talleyrand fell ill. Chills and fever drained his strength. He felt the end approaching. And his beloved Dorothea and Pauline, who were both very religious, began to worry about his soul. They urged him to make his peace with the Church.

Finally he consented and Dorothea hurriedly sent for an abbé whom she had long known and respected. Although this man had never met Talleyrand, Dorothea knew that he had great respect for him, and so she believed that the difficult matter of reconciliation would be smoothly achieved. However, Dorothea was much too hopeful.

Learning from the abbé that Rome demanded a complete admission of error and complete repentance before it would accept him back into the bosom of the Church, Talleyrand resorted to reason and persuasion.

He insisted that he had always been a "child of the Church," and referring to the vows he had broken as priest and bishop, he said that these "errors" had been brought about by the misjudgment of his parents. He said that in entering the Church he had only been obeying the wishes of his parents, and that while he respected their memory "it does not prevent me from saying that all my youth was directed toward a profession for which I was not born."

He went on to say that while he was prepared to make a general admission of guilt, he was not willing to confess to a whole catalogue of crimes. And he suggested that he write

out a paper along these lines which he felt would be acceptable to the Church.

Receiving Talleyrand's "paper," the abbé submitted it to
the proper authorities. But it was not acceptable, and so the
negotiations between the old and dying diplomat and the
Church continued, day after day, week after week.

Dorothea was in the deepest despair. However, when an
agreement was finally reached, Talleyrand delayed signing it.
He delayed and delayed. Until he signed it he could not return to the bosom of the Church, and so Dorothea and
Pauline were filled with dread. He was growing weaker every
day and they feared that he might die without receiving the
last sacrament.

At length on the fifteenth of May, 1838, he realized that his
end was very close. He suffered several attacks of suffocation.
The abbé was called and when little Pauline asked Talleyrand anxiously if he would please sign the paper, he replied,
"Tomorrow between five and six in the morning."

During the night he suffered several more attacks of suffocation. When he was again comfortable, Pauline approached
his bed and asked him, "Uncle, you are calm now. Don't you
want to sign. . . . ?"

"But it is not six o'clock," he replied irritably. "I told you
I would sign between five and six in the morning. I promise
you I will do it then."

The abbé waited together with Dorothea and Pauline,
while Talleyrand dozed fitfully. At five when he awoke, a
little girl dressed all in white and wearing a veil entered and
walked up to his bed. She was the daughter of one of his
cousins, the Baron de Talleyrand, and she was on her way to
church to make her first communion. Her parents had

brought her to Talleyrand's deathbed to receive his bene-
diction.

After she left and when he heard the clock strike six, he
suddenly sat up in bed and said that he was now ready to
sign the paper.

Dorothea brought it and read it to him, slowly and clearly.
He listened carefully, weighing every word, then taking the
pen offered to him and dipping it into the ink, he signed his
name.

At eight o'clock the King, Louis-Philippe, arrived to pay
his last respects.

The old Prince sat up in bed. His mind was perfectly
clear. "It is a great honor that the King does to this house, in
coming here today," he said. Then following court etiquette
he proceeded to present the King to all present.

At ten o'clock the abbé entered the room to administer the
last rites. Talleyrand followed every step with the keenest
interest. When the abbé reached that part of the rites where
the palms of the faithful are anointed with holy oil, Talleyrand held out his two clenched fists, because bishops are
anointed on the back of their hands.

"Do not forget, Monsieur Abbé, that I am a bishop," he
said.

The abbé now fell to his knees and began reciting the pray-
ers for the dead. The murmur of his voice was still audible at
3:35 that afternoon when Talleyrand breathed his last.

Thus came to an end the long life of Charles Maurice de
Talleyrand, a man whom many considered an arch traitor
and evil beyond compare; a man whom others considered the
savior of Europe. Which was he, devil or angel? He was
neither.

The Age of Reason, into which he was born and in which he spent the first twenty-one years of his life, gave him a sense of reality. It laid bare before him the falseness of the feudal concept of society with its serfs and lords and its system of privileges, and inspired him with the ideals of Liberty, Equality and Fraternity. The Revolution, which came upon him when he was thirty-five and had just launched his political career, showed him that long-established social forms could be shattered overnight and that nothing was sacred—everything in society could be questioned, weighed and revised. It taught him that institutions cannot survive when they are out of tune with the times.

Together, the Age of Reason and the Revolution brought him to the realization that man's good, his freedom and dignity, could best be served by a representative form of government. To this belief he remained constant through all the long years of his political career. To this and this alone. And to make his ideal a reality in France, he labored all his life.

Because of his constancy to democratic ideals, Talleyrand was able to survive innumerable historical upheavals. Because of his constancy to the rights of man, he felt free to serve first the Revolution then the Directory; to help make Napoleon and then destroy him; to restore the Bourbons and then overthrow them. Men and governments meant nothing to him. They were only the tools to achieve a goal. For this he has been condemned as corrupt and a traitor.

However, he remained firm in his faith in constitutional government and love for France. The world about him might change, but he remained true to his ideals. When he could serve these causes he did. When conditions were such that he could not further his dream to serve France and liberty, he stepped aside and waited for the government to fall. Then from the ruins he began anew. And if along this rocky road he grew rich, it must be remembered that his immense fortune is greatly outweighed in the scales of history by his services to France.

In short, Talleyrand was neither angel nor devil. He was a man, and subject to the faults of all men. But one thing cannot be denied him. He worked always for man, for the good of France and for the stability and peace of Europe.

About the Author

MANUEL KOMROFF was born in New York City, and educated in schools there and at Yale. He worked as a newspaper ... and during World War I as a war correspondent. His first short stories appeared in 1918, and since then one hundred and thirty of them have been published. He is also the author of many adult novels and biographies of famous historical personages. For a number of years he lectured at Columbia University where he conducted the Novel Writing Workshop. He is a member of the Authors Guild, P.E.N., and the Overseas Press Club.